KT-386-422

SIMPLY◇DIVINE

SIMPLY·DIVINE

—————— Recipes from ——————
The Cooking Canon & Rabbi Blue

BRITISH BROADCASTING CORPORATION

Cover photograph taken by Guglielmo Galvin
at All Saints Vicarage, Bromsgrove, Worcestershire.

China provided by Royal Worcester and garden furniture by
Littleheath Lane Nurseries, Bromsgrove.

Published by the British Broadcasting Corporation,
35 Marylebone High Street, London W1M 4AA

ISBN 0 563 20459 1

First published 1986
© John Eley and Lionel Blue 1986

Set in 9/10 pt Linotron Times Roman by
Wilmaset, Birkenhead, Wirral and printed by
Cox & Wyman Ltd, Reading, Berkshire

Contents

Conversion Tables

All these are approximate conversions which have either
been rounded up or down. Never mix imperial and metric
measures in one recipe, stick to one system or the other.

Oven temperatures

Mark 1	275°F	140°C
2	300°	150°
3	325°	170°
4	350°	180°
5	375°	190°
6	400°	200°
7	425°	220°
8	450°	230°
9	475°	240°

Volume

2 fl oz	55 ml
3	75
5 ($\frac{1}{4}$ pt)	150
$\frac{1}{2}$ pt	275
$\frac{3}{4}$	425
1	570
$1\frac{3}{4}$	1 litre

Measurements

$\frac{1}{8}$ inch	3 mm
$\frac{1}{4}$	$\frac{1}{2}$ cm
$\frac{1}{2}$	1
$\frac{3}{4}$	2
1	2.5
$1\frac{1}{4}$	3
$1\frac{1}{2}$	4
$1\frac{3}{4}$	4.5
2	5
3	7.5
4	10
5	13
6	15
7	18
8	20
9	23
10	25.5
11	28
12	30

Weights

$\frac{1}{2}$ oz	10 g
1	25
$1\frac{1}{2}$	40
2	50
$2\frac{1}{2}$	60
3	75
4	110
$4\frac{1}{2}$	125
5	150
6	175
7	200
8	225
9	250
10	275
12	350
1 lb	450
$1\frac{1}{2}$	700
2	900
3	1 kg 350 g

Dear John,

I was so pleased when you invited me to your home, and even more when you welcomed me into your kitchen. When I entered your front door, I felt an honoured guest, but when I came into your kitchen, I knew we were friends. For us cooks, kitchens are holy, intimate places. I was also curious to meet a vicar and a canon on home ground. I had read a lot about Christianity, but I needed to taste it as well.

As I did not have a Christian education, I only came to the Gospels late in life, but this meant I came to them fresh. What struck me was the intimacy of their stories and how Jewish and culinary they were. Jesus sits in the kitchen of Mary and Martha, he goes to dinner parties with publicans and Pharisees, and he reorganises the catering of a wedding party. I was specially moved by the incident which closes the last Gospel – the fried fish barbecue and breakfast by the shores of the Sea of Galilee. I began to understand why the central act of Christian worship is a meal – a supper, in fact.

And that is something which brings us together. When I came to speak in your church, there was much that was unfamiliar, of course, but there were many things which I had known from earliest childhood, all connected with the blessing of food. On the altar was a cup of wine, and bread on a plate covered with a cloth, flanked by candlesticks. Beside the altar there was a bowl to wash your hands, and a napkin for drying them. These were old, familiar friends, and I realised that the reality of preparing food and giving food unites our faiths and us two personally.

There is a magic about food we all experience – domestic miracles that happen daily. Something sweet soothes a child in an unfamiliar station or airport. A meal whose menu has been composed with tact and consideration blends the different traditions of our multi-faith and pluralist society into a delight. A party where there are loaves and fishes for all is an unplanned festival. And when we welcome the unexpected guest we invite God into our lives.

I should like to say a word about the Jewish food laws. As in most Eastern religions, food and faith are strongly linked. In the West our minds discover God in lectures and books; in the East he comes to us via our taste buds and our kitchen arrangements. My recipes, therefore, do not include forbidden meats such as pork or bacon, or shellfish which is not allowed. Also, milk and meat are not mixed in the same recipe. Non-Jewish readers, who like 'Jewish-style' food, can make their own adjustments. I think our chapter on 'Fancy Religions' is important because the food laws for each religion are complex and intricate. Muslims can eat meat, but shellfish is not forbidden to them as it is with Jews. Hindus will not eat beef. In fact, it is sometimes safest to keep to a vegetarian meal without alcohol, and this can still be delicious.

Sitting in your kitchen after a long journey, with a glass in one hand and a biscuit in the other, I began to count my blessings. The most unexpected of these was becoming a cook, and this has helped me in my ministry. In a kitchen you nourish your soul as well as your body. Trust is created there, and friendship is confirmed with food. The kitchen is a fit place for intimacies, a good confessional, and cook books are its scriptures. It is a holy place, its table an unassuming altar, and both of us clergymen are proud to serve at it, and write for it.

God bless, and thank you,

Lionel.

Dear Lionel,

Thank you very much for coming to share some time with us at All Saints and for giving so much of yourself. It was joy to have you with us and I do hope it will not be too long before you come again.

It does seem that we have a great deal in common, not only the love of breaking bread together but the God that we share. However, the different traditions of our two faiths help make us think, and surely this is a good thing and something that we should use to help us all in our journey through life. I must admit that I am not very knowledgeable on many of the traditions of the great religions when it comes to food, and I certainly look forward to learning more.

It gives me a rather self-indulgent pleasure in inviting different groups of people to share a meal and to observe what goes on as the eating commences. There is also a lot of hard and thoughtful work going on in the kitchen which tends to keep things in perspective. Not being a great academic, I often find myself in situations where I am the host to others whose intellectual achievements far outweigh my own, but it is always a joy to listen and learn from their conversation. I must admit that sometimes the 'chemistry' at my table looks like being disastrous, but the simple act of sharing a meal together does seem to oil the works.

The social gatherings we have in the parish serve well to help keep the community alive in caring for one another and in bringing in those who feel just a little outside the family of the Church. Recently we had a barn dance in the Vicarage garden and eighty-six people had a merry time and enjoyed a little food together. People made new friends and revived old friendships, and at least one long-standing misunderstanding between families was cleared up.

As you know, I place great store on the 'family' side of eating, and firmly believe that families should go out of their way to accommodate each other in sharing at least one simple meal a day. I do sincerely believe that this is important for getting to know each other as individuals and not just taking our own flesh and blood for granted. This carries with it a responsibility for our brothers and sisters of other faiths and countries, and it never ceases to amaze me how generous people are in giving for others as I go about the country presenting charity 'Cook-ins' to help raise funds for various causes. This has become a sort of ministry in itself.

One of the very nice things about going out and about cooking is encouraging others to have another go themselves. I like nothing better than to hear a member of the audience say that he or she feels inspired to go away and cook! Let's hope that this little venture in writing our cookery book will bring many people together and deepen their experience of life and the joy of food and cooking which we both share.

I think we have included something for all tastes and I dare say we have tried to complement each other's palate too. I hope we will share many meals together and keep trying until we get it right!

With every good wish, and happy cooking.
God bless,

1 Fancy Religions

My father was the eldest of a long line of children, and his mother was a hard-working, formidable matriarch of the old school. During the First World War, he was called up for military service, and drafted all over the country from one barracks to another. Wherever he was billeted his mother came too. She would not conceive of separation from her nearest and dearest, and besides her other children, she also brought along a complete kosher kitchen, because she trembled for my father's soul among all that pork and bacon. How she managed to carry it I do not know. Her 'kitchen' was elaborate, with one set of crockery and pans reserved for milk, and another set for meat, and a variety of antiseptics that would have delighted Florence Nightingale, so my father could rinse out his mouth in case . . .

I have used this as an illustration of the importance attached to food in all Eastern religions. In the West, spirituality is theological and mental; in the East it is also cultural and culinary. Western religionists, because of their upbringing, find it difficult to take these gastronomic aspects seriously, and I have noticed very well-disposed clergymen friends smile as Jews, Muslims, Hindus and Sikhs argue passionately about their food laws. A tolerant smile plays around their lips. 'We are understanding,' they seem to be thinking, 'but we know better.'

You have to experience the impact of religion in a kitchen to understand it. You have to feel the purity that bathes the table, when the foods have been prepared not just according to expense, or to your taste, but according to God's will. At the Jewish Sabbath table, the father is a priest, the mother a priestess, and the table is their altar. Is it any wonder that rabbis of old left instructions in their last wills and testaments for their coffins to be made out of the planks of their kitchen tables? It was, they reasoned cogently, the holiest place in their lives, for more blessings had been said over it than anywhere else. When I was told this as a child, I wondered how their widows must have felt, deprived of their husbands and their kitchen tables at

15

one go. But being a wise child, I kept this profane question to myself.

Because Eastern religionists are now our neighbours, and we are commanded to love them, it is not a bad idea to get to know them first. But an ecumenical dinner party does have its problems, and you must take them in your stride with British phlegm. Most of the problems centre round meat so, if you make a vegetarian meal, you cut out most of the problems. Also, if you can, don't put out alcohol. For Sikhs and Muslims, it is really like another form of drug taking, which nibbles away at the free will God gave you and is both forbidden and blasphemous. Take care how you place your guests. A Muslim lady might well prefer not to be separated from her husband though they have been married for more than the customary six months. Don't worry though! Your invitation to your new neighbours will be appreciated, and the God you all worship will dwell among you as a very special guest.

To explain the title of this chapter, I must return to my father in the First World War. At Church Parade, his sergeant bellowed out, 'Fall out all Catholics, and other fancy religions!' Jews were pretty fancy at that time, but they have since been joined by others even fancier.

Lionel Blue

Epiphany Pâté   L.B.

Aubergines, with their bulbous shape and shiny purple skin, look exotic on the greengrocer's shelf. They have two drawbacks for the cook. They absorb oil like blotting paper, and some people don't like their bitter juice, so they cut them, salt them and drain them before cooking.

This recipe avoids both problems. The aubergines are baked not fried and I don't taste any bitterness, only a smokiness which is interesting and makes me want more. It is an hors d'oeuvre which goes well with sesame biscuits, or crackers, or Greek pitta bread, or toast. It will remind you of romance, and little Mediterranean cafés, and your last package holiday, and it may remind your Eastern guests of home. The three wise men would have liked it, so I have called it Epiphany Pâté.

2 large aubergines	1 small onion
(1¾–2 lbs)	½ tsp sugar
1 large onion	1 tsp salt
2 cloves garlic	12 grinds pepper
3 tbsp olive oil	Tomatoes, olives and
1 tbsp lemon juice	parsley for garnishing

Prick the aubergines with a fork, and bake them in a hot oven for about an hour at gas mark 6, 400°F (200°C), until they are soft and wrinkled. Peel and chop the onion and garlic and fry them in the olive oil until brown.

When the aubergines are cooked, skin them. Mix together in a food processor the aubergine flesh and all the other ingredients except the small raw onion. Chop this finely and fold into the aubergine mixture.

Cooked aubergine has a greyish look, so decorate with slices of red tomato, green and black olives, and chopped parsley.

Beetroot in Jelly   J.E.

A visit to Vera Stewart's table in Carlisle has always been full of gastronomic surprises. This simple vegetable dish is one which delighted me and a few other clerics when we met there for a feast a few years ago. I enjoy it with a good deal of black pepper and brown bread and butter, and of course it is particularly suitable for a bishop or cardinal, considering the colour. Serves 8.

1-lb jar of cubed beetroot	½ pint boiling water
1 pint-sized pkt red jelly or	
blackcurrant jelly	

Simply boil a kettle full of water and measure out ½ pint onto the jelly. When all the jelly has been dissolved add the juice from the beetroot to the liquid jelly and make up to about ¾ pint of liquid.

Place the cubed beetroot in a suitable container and pour on the jelly and beetroot liquid. Allow to set and then chill well before serving by placing it in the fridge for about an hour.

To remove the jelly from its container let it stand momentarily in a bowl of warm water and then turn out onto a bed of finely chopped watercress or lettuce.

Mushroom Cups   L.B.

A few Eastern religionists do have problems with milk products. Some Hindus feel that cow's milk is meant for the calf not for them. And a strong-smelling cheese once horrified a Buddhist friend of mine from Thailand – it seemed to him so rank. Some vegans, who are stricter than ordinary vegetarians, have the same problems.

Yet I think most fancy religionists, whether Jewish, Muslim, Hindu or Sikh, will get pleasure without problems from this simple but elegant dish. Mushrooms and aubergines are the nearest equivalents to meat among the vegetables, in texture and taste.

To make 8 bread cups, lightly butter on both sides 8 slices of decrusted bread (brown or white). Push them into individual Yorkshire pudding tins or deep tart tins, and bake them in a hot preheated oven, gas mark 5, 375°F (190°C), for 15 minutes. They should then be crisp, browned, and keep their cup shape.

To fill the bread cups, take:

$\frac{1}{2}$ lb mushrooms, sliced	2 tbsp snipped spring onion
3 tbsp butter	greens or chives
3 tbsp flour	1 tbsp lemon juice
1 tsp salt	1 tbsp chopped parsley
8 oz single cream or rather	Sprinkle of paprika
less double cream	

Sauté the sliced mushrooms in the butter for 5 minutes. Take the pan off the heat, and stir in the flour, and then the cream. Season. Add the spring onion greens. Cook gently until the mixture thickens. Add the lemon juice.

Serve warm in the bread cases, and sprinkle with parsley and paprika. I have left out a dessertspoon of sherry to avoid any problem with alcohol. On your own, of course, you might not be so disciplined.

Aubergine and Potato Bake   J.E.

To be quite honest, I have never really had to do much
ecumenical entertaining that has involved paying special
attention to food laws. Even the most conservative of
tastes and strictest of rules can no doubt be settled quite
simply with a little thought and planning. This savoury
dish is indeed one which I enjoy myself so it is never a real
sacrifice to offer it at the table to those who do not relish
their meat as much as I do. Serves 6.

2 large aubergines	1 tsp dried basil
2 lb potatoes	12 oz grated cheddar
2 large onions	cheese
1 lb tomatoes	Salt and black pepper

Wash and slice the aubergines and sprinkle them with a
little salt and allow them to 'sweat'. This will allow the
excess water to be released. Wipe the aubergines dry and
arrange a few slices on the bottom of an ovenproof dish.
  Fry the sliced onions in some oil until they are soft. Boil
the washed and peeled potatoes in some lightly salted
water for 10 minutes and slice them up. Slice the tomatoes.
  Now build up layers in the dish of aubergines, onion,
potato, tomato and spinkle each layer with grated cheese.
Season each layer of tomato with the dried basil. Season
with salt and pepper. Cover and bake in the oven at gas
mark 5, 375°F (190°C), for 1½ hours until it is golden
brown.
  Serve immediately with a green salad.

Buddha's Bolognese   L.B.

This recipe was passed on to me by a friend, as all the best
recipes are. In fact a recipe is one of the nicest presents to
receive. I tried it out on some Buddhists who gave it
unstinted approval.
  I say this with relief, because at a previous dinner party,
a Buddhist monk had been my guest. He was a most
courteous man. Though he did not speak a word of any

language my other guests could muster, he smiled sweetly and interestedly throughout their chatter, and I gather he enjoyed himself. It took some time, however, for the guests to accept his presence naturally, for he sat about three feet from the table, with his bowl in front of him. Bits were put in the bowl, and as he ate them all with no hint of displeasure, I presume he liked my cooking.

Until I had detached myself from all thought of social success and failure, I found the situation wearing. But, after I ceased to bother, I found my peace, and both of us appeared to enjoy each other's company for we smiled amiably at each other through the rest of the meal without any other contact.

For 4 Buddhists you must have: 1 lb of fresh, cooked pasta. I like using the green flat noodles made with spinach. Make sure it stays hot after cooking, by keeping it in a colander over simmering water.

For the sauce, you will require:

½ lb courgettes, thinly sliced
½ lb button mushrooms,
  roughly chopped
3 tbsp parsley
1 large onion, chopped
1 large clove garlic,
  chopped
2 tbsp olive oil
1 tbsp fresh basil or 1 tsp
  dried basil

4 oz tomato purée (not the
  concentrate)
2–3 oz slivered almonds or
  pine nuts to give protein
Pinch of sugar
Salt and lots of freshly
  ground black pepper

As the ingredients are simple they should also be the best. So please use fresh pasta, fresh herbs if possible, and good-quality olive oil.

Sweat the onion and garlic in the olive oil. Add the courgettes and mushrooms, with a little salt and lots of freshly ground pepper, and the parsley and basil. Cook very slowly for 30 minutes, and then stir in the tomato purée and sugar.

Cook for another 30 minutes, until the mixture is thick and rich and fragrant. Add slivered almonds or pine nuts 5 minutes before the end.

Pour the sauce over the pasta, and combine both gently, not violently, as the Buddha would have approved.

Savoury Cauliflower Bake   J.E.

The great thing about a cauliflower cheese is that it can be
served as a vegetable for some and a main course for
others without anyone noticing who is taking what. This
simple recipe saves all sorts of complications in ecumenical
eating.

I really do enjoy this recipe which was once prepared for
me by a family of Buddhists and we had a delicious green
salad to accompany it. In fact, each week I do try to have
one meatless day and this is often one of the dishes on my
menu. Serves 6.

1 large cauliflower	6 oz strong cheddar cheese,
6 oz mushrooms	grated
2 oz butter	2 tbsp double cream
¼ pint milk	Salt and pepper

Cut the cauliflower into quarters and cook until tender in
lightly salted water, simmering gently. Melt the butter in a
pan and add the finely chopped mushrooms, cooking
gently until they are tender. Season with salt and pepper.
Stir in the milk and grated cheese and bring this to the boil
for a couple of minutes.

Place the cooked cauliflower in a warmed serving dish
and pour over the rich sauce to which has been added the
cream at the last minute. Pop under a hot grill for a couple
of minutes to brown.

Colcannon   L.B.

Everyone in Ireland has his or her own recipe for
Colcannon. 'This is how me own mother made it, and
don't let them tell you different now, for I was a country
girl, mind!' Well, to increase the confusion, here is a
rabbi's version to join those of the Irish mothers. This is a
true peasant dish, and you will find it in kitchens but not so
easily in gourmet restaurants. It's lovely, but lowly.

For 3 people you will need:

1 lb potatoes (the flourier the better)	5 fat spring onions
	Teacup of rich milk
¾ lb kale if you can get it, or green cabbage or spring greens if you can't	2 tbsp chopped parsley
	2 oz butter
	Salt and pepper

Cut the stalks out of the kale or cabbage, and boil the leaves rapidly in salted boiling water for not more than 5 minutes. They should be cooked but firm. Press the water out when draining.

Peel the potatoes and boil them until cooked in salted water. While they are boiling, cut up the spring onions and parsley into a teacup of milk. Add 1 ounce of butter, 1 teaspoon of salt and ¼ teaspoon of pepper, and heat until it is just about to simmer.

Drain the potatoes, and mash them. Put them back in the pan. Chop the greens finely and add to the potatoes. Now add the hot milk with the onions and parsley to the pan. Add another tablespoon of butter, and mash away like mad over a very gentle heat.

You will now have a lovely fluffy green dotted mash. Serve it hot with more melted butter.

Coffee Walnut Ice Cream   J.E.

Americans do make delicious sweet and gooey things. This simple ice cream was given to me by some American friends who in their spare time flew B-52 bombers, 'just to keep them occupied'! They were more interested in seeing Britain and enjoying life here, and shared with us some of their culinary delights.

If you do have an ice cream machine then this is one of the nicest ice creams that you can make in it. I once had a Quaker family to breakfast and the only thing the children wanted was ice cream. This one kept them blissfully quiet. Serves 6.

¾ pint double cream	¾ pint water
6 oz castor sugar	3 tbsp instant coffee
4 oz chopped walnuts	1 tbsp honey

Heat the water and dissolve the coffee, sugar and honey. Allow to cool. Add the chopped nuts and the double cream to the pan and mix well.

Pour into a plastic container and freeze for an hour before beating with a wooden spoon and then freezing again and beating again so that the water icicles are beaten out and the ice cream is smooth.

Delicious with langue de chat biscuits, and a little cream.

Honey Glazed Fruit J.E.

Fruit on its own is delicious and makes a splendid end to any meal with the minimum of fuss and preparation. I first heard about this recipe from someone who had been for a world cruise aboard one of those luxury liners which we would all like to travel the world on. Their selection of possible fruits was obviously more exotic than what we have available throughout the year, but with careful selection and care, the little of what we do have can in fact be superb.

I tend to use fruits with skins but if you are very clever you can use certain fine soft fruits as well, and all benefit from being consumed on the day of making. If you worshipped Isis or Osiris you might well be tempted to live off honey and fruit. What better way than this? These quantities serve 6 if you want to be greedy.

6 tbsp clear honey
12 oz castor sugar

An assortment of fresh fruit, e.g. peeled tangerines, red and white grapes, cherries etc . . .

Heat the sugar and honey in a thick saucepan and allow the sugar to dissolve without stirring. Bring gently to the boil and keep boiling until a hard ball is formed when the mixture is dropped into a saucer of cold water. This is at 320°F (160°C) on a sugar thermometer.

Having washed the fruit and carefully dried every piece, quickly dip the fruit in the very hot solution using a fork and then place on some wire racks to cool and set.

Arrange the glazed fruit in a glass serving bowl. This dish must be kept in a cool and dry atmosphere.

2 What the Actress Fed the Bishop

My contact with actresses and bishops has never been such that we have had time to discuss either what the actress would desire to feed the bishop, or what the bishop has been fed by any particular actress. I must confess that I have had far more contact with actresses than with bishops, but then there are rather more of them than there are bishops.

The first real stage star I ever met was Dulcie Gray. Michael Denison and Dulcie had come to the Theatre Royal in Bury St Edmunds to present a programme of Shakespearian sonnets to help raise funds for the restoration of the theatre. One night Dulcie came off the stage with a tear in her eye having read a very moving sonnet. Being the gallant young lad that I was I offered her my clean handkerchief . . . and I have still got it to this day! There have been other 'encounters' with actresses but they will have to wait for another occasion!

I have always admired bishops, but for very different reasons. In the main they are both hospitable and fiercely caring for their clergy. In fact bishops are in many ways the people I feel for most in the Church. They are the true pastors while we clergy flood them with administrative office work.

When I worked on local radio I was always popping in to see bishops from every denomination, and it used to amuse me when they all seemed to ask, 'What do you want me to say?' What an opportunity to influence the face of the Church, as if I, the humble interviewer, really knew the answers! But it was usually a sign of their humility that they wanted to make their point in a way that listeners would understand.

When he came to this country in 1982, I believe the Pope ate heartily of all the regional dishes that were offered to him and this does seem to have given many people a tremendous thrill. But what would an actress give him to eat, let alone a rabbi? I'm not quite sure if all actresses would choose what we have chosen, but we have tried to find recipes that would appeal to people who wish to share the pleasures of the table with special friends and

25

experience the joy which eating together can bring – and perhaps share the similarities in each other's world and professions. After all, both actresses and bishops do need to have a little knowledge of showbiz!

John Eley

Gorgonzola Pâté   J.E.

There are times when the palate needs a bit of a shock to wake it up. So too does the tired prelate after a day dealing with all his clergy. This will revive your interest in food and flavour after a tiring day, and sees any dinner party off to a good start. In larger quantities, it goes down well as a dip with sliced cucumber, carrots and celery. Serves 6.

4 oz Gorgonzola cheese	1 oz flour
6 black olives	1 pint milk
1 tbsp mayonnaise	$\frac{1}{4}$ tsp cayenne pepper
1 clove garlic	1 tbsp gin
1 tbsp soured cream	Avocado or tomatoes
1 oz butter	

In a thick, small saucepan blend the flour and butter and heat gently, then gradually add the milk to make a thickish white sauce. You may need a little more milk but the sauce must be left to set when it is cool.

In a food processor or liquidiser place the cheese, garlic, mayonnaise, stoned black olives, soured cream, cayenne pepper and the gin and process for a couple of minutes. Add the white sauce and process once again. Put the mixture in a bowl and cover with some plastic film. Place in the fridge to chill and set.

In the meantime prepare either an avocado or some tomatoes by removing the respective stone or seeds. When the pâté has set, spoon it into a piping bag with a small star nozzle and pipe the mixture into the cavities of the avocado or tomato. Sprinkle a little cayenne pepper on the top just before serving. The pâté needs to be kept well chilled at all times.

As an alternative you may like to use Stilton and replace the olives with some chopped walnuts after the final processing. Leave out the gin and use port instead. This style of pâté is delicious with hot, crispy brown rolls.

Light Liver   L.B.

This recipe is excellent for a tête-à-tête. I do not know what the actress and the bishop are discussing, perhaps theology, who knows? At parties I often get buttonholed by people who ask me about eternal life, Biblical criticism and such matters.

Anyway, whatever they are discussing – and it is not right to pry, or 'make windows into people's souls' – they will need something light to nourish their communication, something they can toy with, and linger over. Perhaps the actress will put a piece of the pâté on a biscuit, and coyly pass it to the bishop.

These quantities will give the two of them ample quantities to toy with:

½ lb chicken livers, carefully cleaned and any dark globules removed
1 medium onion, sliced
2 tbsp chicken fat, or margarine, or vegetarian 'chicken' fat called Mazchik

4 eggs beaten with 2 tbsp water
1 small raw onion, very finely chopped
Chives to garnish
Salt and freshly ground pepper

Fry the sliced onion gently in half the fat until soft. Add the livers to the pan. Season and continue frying until the livers are soft. In a mincer or food processor grind the contents of the pan.

Now scramble the beaten eggs in the same pan with the rest of the fat. Mix the scrambled eggs with the livers until you have a fluffy paste. Mix in the raw onion, put in a pretty pot, and garnish with chives. You can serve it on toast or biscuits. Or you can serve it on celery or carrot sticks, if either actress or bishop are on a diet.

When I lived in Carlisle fresh salmon used to mysteriously appear on my doorstep at the most peculiar hours, but always in prime condition. So, with what seemed to be an abundant supply, I was able to experiment and this recipe was the result of one of those tests. I even managed to encourage a young actress to share a simple meal at my table, and since both the actress and the salmon arrived on the same day, I had no excuse not to feed her this noble fish. These quantities will serve 4.

4 salmon steaks or fillets	5 fluid oz soured cream
2 oz butter	2 tbsp freshly chopped
1 bay leaf	chives
1 shallot	1 oz plain flour
5 fluid oz fish stock	Black pepper

Spread half the butter over an ovenproof dish and place the salmon steaks or fillets neatly in, sprinkling with the chopped shallot and half the chopped chives. Place the bay leaf in the centre of the dish and add the fish stock and a little black pepper. Dot the remaining butter over the salmon, cover the dish with foil and bake in the centre of an oven set at gas mark 5, 375°F (190°C), for about 20 minutes. The aim is to cook the salmon gently so if you decide to use a 'hot' stock, take a little time off the cooking.

In the meantime blend the flour with a little water to make a weak paste. When cooked, remove the salmon from the dish and wrap in foil to keep warm. If you are using salmon steaks remove the skin and the bones from the fish at this stage.

Add the flour and water to the juices left in the pan and allow them to simmer on the top of the stove until the flour is cooked and the sauce thickens. Add the rest of the chives and a little water if necessary before stirring in the soured cream when you have removed the dish from the heat. Adjust the seasoning if necessary.

To serve, heat a large oval or rectangular meat dish and pour in the delicious sauce, then carefully arrange the salmon in the sauce without covering it. Sprinkle on some freshly chopped chives.

This is absolutely irresistible with French bread, green salad and a good white wine.

Mexican food is fiery, and because the Mexicans are accustomed to it, they can nonchalantly munch a chilli with its seeds as they saddle their 'burro'. But though you long for authenticity (a favourite word of theological students, though I can't work out what it means), it is better to tone down the truth and serve an inauthentic English version instead. This recipe will serve both the actress and the bishop very well, for it will heat up their relationship without burning their innards. The dish is better made in advance, to give the chilli time to transform itself into a gentle warmth, which will make the avocados glow. If you put clingfilm over the pot or the avocado shells, they will not discolour.

These quantities should be ample for both the actress and the bishop, and even if their understudy or dean should join them, there will be sufficient.

1 large ripe avocado	1 tsp salt
2 hard-boiled eggs	6 grinds black pepper
½ deseeded chilli	Pinch of sugar
1 quite small onion or ½ a medium-sized one	2 tbsp yoghurt
	Juice of ½ lemon
2 cloves garlic	

Cut the avocado in two, removing the stone. Take out the flesh carefully and mash it with the lemon juice. Roughly chop the eggs. Finely chop the onion. Mince the chilli and garlic. Mix them all together with the avocado flesh and the remaining ingredients.

Pile the mixture into the avocado shells, and cover with clingfilm. Chill.

Serve garnished with tomato quarters and corn chips.

I am not sure if we have any bishops left in the Church of England who sport the Grouse Moor image, but I do know the odd hunting parson and a solicitor who is a priest and keeps a pack of beagles, so the chances are there is a cardinal who enjoys his pheasant. To this noble personage I dedicate this dish . . . and if it is cooked by an actress, well then, all the better! Serves 4.

Brace of fine pheasants	2 tbsp redcurrant jelly
2 oz butter	1 wineglassful of good
2 tbsp olive oil	brandy
12 small onions	1 bay leaf
24 lightly roasted chestnuts	1 large orange
2 level tbsp flour	Salt and black pepper
½ bottle good burgundy	

If you are able to have your pheasants dressed by your game supplier you will not regret it! Having successfully achieved this, wash the birds thoroughly and wipe them dry before seasoning with a little salt and black pepper. Use a large, thick and deep casserole to melt the butter and oil together until they are nearly foaming and then, using two large forks to turn them, brown the pheasants thoroughly on every side. Remove the birds from the pot and carefully fry the onions in the same pot until they are browning nicely. Remove the onions and keep on one side with the pheasants.

Add the flour to the pan and allow it to cook for about a minute before gently adding the redcurrant jelly and wine to make a thickish sauce. Grate in the rind of the orange and the juice together with the bay leaf. Return the pheasants and onions to the pot and add the chestnuts. Heat the brandy in a ladle before setting fire to it and pouring it onto the pheasants. Let it burn out and adjust the seasoning. Place on a well-fitting lid and if you wish to make a better seal place a layer of greaseproof paper over the top before fitting the lid.

Place in the centre of an oven set at gas mark 4, 350°F (180°C), and allow to cook for 1½–2 hours. The aroma whilst cooking is delicious and I sometimes add a few coriander seeds to give that little extra!

As a vegetable accompaniment I suggest the following when there are new potatoes around:

1 lb sliced new potatoes	4 oz smoked streaky bacon
4 oz butter	Salt and black pepper

In an ovenproof dish spread some of the butter and place a layer of the sliced potatoes. Cut the bacon into thinnish strips and add a layer to the potatoes and so on until they are all used up, making sure that you finish with a layer of potatoes on the top. Sprinkle each layer with a little salt and black pepper and finally dot the rest of the butter on the top.

Place the dish in the oven about an hour before you serve the pheasants, and cook at the top of the oven at gas mark 4, 350°F (180°C). This is a lovely way to serve potatoes as a change, especially with the Sunday roast.

French Almond Tart with Choristers' Cream   J.E.

A deliciously simple pudding, but it must be eaten on the day of preparation and preferably within hours. I somehow think this is the dish that an actress might like to feed a bishop. There is something very moreish about warm almond paste and puff pastry and the cream, of course, makes it heavenly . . . Serves 6.

12 oz puff pastry	2 eggs
2 oz butter	2 tbsp rum
6 oz ground almonds	2 drops almond essence
6 oz castor sugar	

Divide the puff pastry into two and roll out and cut into two 10-inch rounds. Use a dinner plate or a flan tin as a guide.

To make the paste, gently warm the butter so that it is soft and with a wooden spoon blend together all the ingredients. If it is too soft it may be advisable to let the paste chill in a refrigerator for a few minutes to firm up a little.

With a well-beaten egg brush one of the discs of puff pastry. With the tip of a sharp knife make indentations in the pastry disc from the centre using a curving action as if making curved spokes in a wheel.

Spoon the almond paste mixture into the centre of the pastry disc that has not been 'inscribed' and brush the edges well with the beaten egg. Place the 'inscribed' disc over the almond paste-filled disc. Press the edges down very firmly and brush the top with beaten egg and sprinkle with castor sugar.

Place in the centre of an oven set at gas mark 7, 425°F (220°C), for about 20 minutes until risen and golden brown. Allow to cool until 'warm' before serving with spoonfuls of 'Choristers' Cream'.

Choristers' Cream

5 fluid oz double cream	1 oz castor sugar
1 large egg white	1 drop vanilla essence

Lightly whip the double cream. Whisk the cool egg white until it peaks. Fold in the castor sugar and essence to the egg white and then fold this mixture into the double cream. Do make sure that it is well blended. Chill well but eat within 4 hours of being made. A delicious and light way to serve cream, it is also a little more economical. Spoon it on lavishly.

Sabayon Strawberries   L.B.

I normally dislike dishes which have to be cooked at the last moment. They make me edgy, and I can't enjoy my own party. Sabayon sauce is an exception because it is docile and if you make simple preparations there are no nasty surprises. It costs a lot in a restaurant, but very little if you make it yourself.

For 4 people you will need:

1 lb strawberries	4 tbsp castor sugar
4 tbsp icing sugar	4 tbsp sweet sherry or any
4 large egg yolks (you can	other sweet fortified wine
use the whites for	such as port or madeira
meringues)	

You will need the following implements:

- an electric hand-held beater
- a saucepan half-full with simmering water
- a bowl which fits into the saucepan and sits on its rim
- 4 large wine glasses or tumblers.

Hull the strawberries, cut them in half, and dust them with the icing sugar. Divide them among the 4 glasses. Chill in the fridge.

When the main course is being served, put the saucepan on the stove to simmer. It should start to simmer when you are collecting up the main course plates. Now you have to work speedily but not recklessly.

In the bowl put the egg yolks, castor sugar, and fortified wine. Rest the bowl on the rim of the saucepan half-filled with water, simmering on the stove. Beat the contents of the bowl immediately with the electric beater, without stopping. (If you only have a manual beater, make rice pudding or something else instead.)

The egg wine mixture will gradually increase in bulk and thickness (about 6–7 minutes). When it holds its shape like whipped cream, turn off the heat, lift the bowl out, and spoon the Sabayon into the 4 glasses over the strawberries. Serve immediately.

Two cautions! If you beat too long, you will get scrambled eggs. If you don't serve immediately, and let the sauce cool, the egg and wine will separate. But don't be frightened, it is easy enough and one practice makes perfect. It is really a very superior custard, and much more interesting with strawberries than any cream, except perhaps real clotted cream from Cornwall.

Ascension Soufflé   J.E.

I was once asked back several times by a television producer to present some cookery items at certain times of the Ecclesiastical year. Christmas, Easter and Whitsun provided very few problems but Ascensiontide took a little bit of tongue-in-cheek courage and so I dreamt up this lemon mint soufflé. It has a delicious flavour but the soured cream gives one the feeling that a little something has left . . . ascended even! Serves 6.

6 large lemons	1 dessertspoon freshly
8 large eggs	chopped lemon mint
8 oz castor sugar	1 heaped tbsp gelatine
$\frac{3}{4}$ pint double cream	A little hot water
$\frac{1}{4}$ pint soured cream	

First, soften the gelatine by following the instructions on the packet. Then chop the mint, having selected a decent-looking sprig for decoration. Stir the chopped mint into the soured cream and leave for an hour or so.

Separate the eggs and cover the whites with some plastic film. Store them in the fridge until you need them.

Place the egg yolks in a large bowl and add the castor sugar and squeeze in the juice of the lemons. Do not throw all the rind away just at the moment. Whisk the yolks, sugar and lemon juice together until the mixture is light and fluffy. Then place this bowl inside a large pan of simmering water, add the softened gelatine and keep whisking gently until the mixture begins to thicken. To achieve this use either a hand or balloon whisk. When you feel it has thickened enough, place the mixture to one side out of the hot water.

Beat the double cream and whisk the egg whites separately until they are really very stiff. Blend together the soured cream and double cream and then blend this with the lemon mixture. Do make sure that they are well mixed. Then *fold* this mixture into the whisked egg whites using a figure-of-eight movement with a metal spoon.

Prepare a large soufflé dish, a $1\frac{1}{2}$-pint size should be large enough, but you will need to place a collar around the soufflé dish of greaseproof paper which rises at least 3 inches above the edge of the soufflé dish to hold in the mixture. This gives the soufflé that marvellous 'risen' effect when you remove the collar. Pour in the mixture and allow to set for at least 3 hours. If you do place it in the fridge make sure that you cover the top with a little plastic film so that a tough skin will not form on the top.

When the soufflé has set, decorate the top with some finely grated rind of lemon and that reserved piece of lemon mint. To remove the paper collar successfully, wet a palette knife and gently ease it around the soufflé between the paper and the mixture. Then remove the paper with care.

A refreshingly tasty end to a meal.

34

3 A Little of What You Fancy

I only began to enjoy eating on my own as I grew older. When I was younger I needed to be part of the group, a member of the herd, and solo cooking seemed to be only for failures.

Well, if you feel a failure, your cooking reflects it. In my bedsitter, I used to end up with a tin of baked beans, and the final sign of defeat was to eat them straight out of a tin with a spoon. Actually, cold baked beans taste rather nice, and should never be despised because they are full of protein. But at the time, I had too much self-pity to see this, and sometimes I cried into the can which spoilt the beans and made them salty.

It was a pity I was so morose and adolescent because I could have had a good time in my own company, and years later there is nothing I long for more than a quiet supper alone, when I don't have to make conversation and can sit in my favourite chair next to the gramophone. If you are alone, you can eat all the foods you really like, not the foods you ought to like. I am partial to many things not found in a good food guide. I like tinned pilchards, and cold custard. I enjoy raw onions, and butties made with milk chocolate. I have my secret tipple of Worcestershire sauce, flavoured with tomato, and if I like something, I like a lot of it. Most people have their own secret list of likes, but not many confess to the items. An exception is my mother who enjoys, above all things, advocaat mixed with cherry brandy and topped with whipped cream. This concoction she eats out of an egg cup with a teaspoon.

It was religion which changed my attitude to solo eating. One miserable New Year's Eve in a foreign town, a very obvious fact occurred to me. As God is everywhere, nobody is ever alone, if you invite His company. I did invite Him and I've never really eaten alone since. That is a reliable miracle of religion, to change a loneliness you loathe into a solitude you love.

People have different fancies. I like simple recipes which release me from work and worry. For John richness is all, even if he has to work hard for it. Our tables are according to our temperaments, and I think you will find that the recipes we have chosen reflect this.

Lionel Blue

King Prawns Wrapped in Bacon J.E.

I am undoubtedly one of the worst people for ordering a meal in a restaurant and then spending the rest of the meal wishing I had ordered what the person opposite has so wisely decided upon. One day I had obviously given the game away as I sat, almost green with envy, looking at those plump king prawns on that far-off plate. I did not even look at the person who was eating them until he speared a prawn with his fork and gave it to me. The worst thing was that I was right – I should have ordered what he had had. These prawns are delicious . . . try them. Serves 4.

12 king prawns	6 oz butter
(3 per person)	2 cloves garlic
12 bacon rashers	

Fire the king prawns under a hot grill until they are cooked. If you are buying frozen ones you should find specific instructions on the packet. Remove the prawns from their shells and wrap them in some very thin smoked bacon and, thus wrapped, cook them quickly under the grill until the bacon is cooked.

Crush the garlic into a thick saucepan and add the butter. Heat it until the butter has melted.

Divide the prawns between 4 heated plates and pour over the garlic butter.

Serve with hot French bread.

Self-Pity Meatballs L.B.

These meatballs were refugees from Sweden. They journeyed across the Atlantic to the States, and then journeyed back to Europe, so although this recipe has a Scandinavian basis, when it reached me it had acquired an American kick, which I toned down because of my British understatement. It is very easy and very versatile. It is good both for solo cooking, and for party cooking when all the tribes of Israel descend on me. When I am on my own for too long, I get lachrymose. These balls sauce me up, and I decide that life is worth living, and I even get down to prayer – my first for some time – and I just say 'Thank you!'

I give here the quantities for one large portion. It is enough for one self-pitying rabbi or two normal people. Multiply the quantity according to the number of your guests and their emotions.

½ lb mince
4 fluid oz tomato juice
  (½ a small tin)
4 fluid oz ketchup
  (½ a small bottle)

1 tbsp redcurrant jelly
1 dessertspoon lemon juice
½ tsp made-up English
  mustard

Wet your hands, and roll the mince into balls, the size of small walnuts.

In a saucepan combine all the other ingredients except the lemon juice. Heat on the stove until it is just simmering.

Carefully put the balls in the simmering sauce, and cook very slowly over a low heat for a long time (40 minutes at least, but longer will be better).

Before serving add lemon juice to taste. This will moderate the sauce, which is very rich. You will not need any extra salt or pepper.

I like to eat the sauced balls with rye bread, especially the Jewish type, which is worth seeking out because it is flecked with caraway seeds, a taste I enjoy.

Sole Colbert J.E.

Colbert was a powerful minister in the Court of Louis XIV and there are several rich French dishes named after him. There is no doubt about it, you do have to be rich to afford Dover sole in a restaurant these days, but this dish can easily be cooked by anyone. It takes more time than you would think to prepare but there are more and more semi-prepared sole appearing on the market and provided they are cooked correctly they are a delight. Serves 4.

4 sole weighing about 8 oz each, skinned

Coating	*Maître d'hôtel Butter*
4 oz wholemeal flour	4 oz butter
4 oz brown breadcrumbs	2 tsp lime juice
½ tsp salt	1 tbsp chopped parsley
½ tsp black pepper	Salt and black pepper
2 large eggs	
2 tbsp oil	

A large number of supermarkets are selling first-class Dover sole and they come fresh and ready dressed as far as being beheaded and skinned goes. You will, however, need to remove the backbone which is particularly strong in this fish. Fortunately, this really is not too difficult. First, and most important of all, you will need a really *sharp* knife.

Place the fish on a wooden cutting board and using the sharp knife make an incision down the middle of the flat side of the fish and then pick up the fish and bend it almost in half. This will serve to expose the bone and then using firm but continuous strokes begin to pare the flesh away from the bones. With a little firm handling the bone should soon be removed. Repeat this process for each fish. By the time that you have come to the last fish, the chances are that you will have got it right. Now to prepare the coating. Mix together with a fork the flour, the breadcrumbs, and a little salt and pepper. Beat the eggs and the oil together.

With a large pastry brush liberally coat the fish on each side and in the cavity made by the removal of the backbone. Fold back the meat eased off the backbone and make sure you have coated it well. Then firmly press on the flour and breadcrumb mixture.

When all the fish are well coated place on a tray and chill well in the fridge. They can be prepared a few hours in advance before cooking.

Now prepare the maître d'hôtel butter by gently blending together the butter, lime juice, chopped parsley and a little salt and pepper.

To cook the fish you need a large deep frying pan and usually, because of the size of the fish, I use one of my

'French' casserole pans and a thermometer to check the temperature of the quality cooking oil that I like to use. Sole is really too expensive to make mistakes with so do check the temperature of the oil very carefully: 350°F (180°C) on a frying thermometer.

Cook each fish for 6 minutes by which time they should be golden brown. You will need to make sure there is room in the oven to keep them warm on a pre-warmed container. After all the fish is cooked, pipe on a little of the maître d'hôtel butter into the cavity left by the removal of the backbone and sprinkle with finely chopped parsley.

Serve immediately with fresh green vegetables and new potatoes.

Poor Fish   L.B.

If the poor fish is a kipper, then you are not a poor fish at all. Only when humble herrings have become scarce, and tins of them in tomato sauce can only be bought in Harrods, will their quality and sheer good taste be recognised. And of all the ways of preparing herrings, the British smoked kipper is the best. It was, and still is, the smoked salmon of the poor. Kipper is so good that it needs the least cooking possible and in this way of preparing it, you don't cook the fish, but let the lemon juice do it for you.

For 1 greedy person you will need:

1 boned kipper fillet	1 tbsp olive oil
Fresh or bottled lemon juice to cover	(flavourings and spices optional)

Lay the kipper fillet flat and skin side up in a glass dish. Cover completely and generously with lemon juice. Add the oil. Cover the dish with a lid, foil or clingfilm and leave in the fridge overnight.

Take out the kipper, and throw away the marinade. Pat the kipper dry. With care, the skin comes off quite easily, and you will have 2 fillets in all. Serve with thin slices of raw onion and tomato. (If you make this dish for company 1 fillet per person is quite enough.)

You can flavour the marinade by putting any of the following in with the kipper, alone or in combination: a deseeded chilli, coriander seeds, cardamom pods, pepper-corns. Kipper is so rich, I usually just give it an unperfumed lemon juice bath.

Eat it with good-quality cottage loaf, or wholemeal bread.

Fillet Steak Whisky Galore   J.E.

My recent travels have taken me to the delightful area of Speyside in Scotland, with its beautiful countryside peppered with distilleries and fields full of lush pasture and fine-looking beasts. What a wonderful combination these two make in this flavoursome dish! Serves 4.

4 prime fillet steaks	½ lb field mushrooms
¾ pint double cream	2 shallots
2 measures of fine malt	2 oz butter
whisky liqueur	Salt and black pepper

At least two weeks before you need them, order your fillet steaks and make sure that they come from a beast that has been well hung. On the morning of the cooking, if it is early spring, rise early and gather your field mushrooms from the meadows. Failing that, go to your enlightened greengrocer and choose some of the freshest that you can find.

Using a thick frying pan, melt a little of the butter, add some salt and pepper and cook the steaks to your liking. I prefer to have my meat very raw, which is not to everyone's taste, but please do not turn this delicious meat from a noble beast into a burnt offering. When cooked to your liking, remove the meat from the pan and keep covered and warm in an oven.

Melt the rest of the butter in the same frying pan and add the chopped shallots and cook until they are soft but not brown. Finely chop the mushrooms into small cubes and add to the pan after the onion has cooked. Pour in the whisky and heat and flame! When the flames die down remove from the heat and stir in the cream. Return the pan to a gentle heat and allow the sauce – which may benefit from a little black pepper – to thicken a little.

To serve, make rounds of fresh fried bread, place each steak on one and spoon over a portion of the sauce.

The partridge has the most delicate flavour of all the game birds and serves as the best introduction to the pleasures of the game larder for the beginner. In fact I know some seasoned ladies who will not eat any other kind of game bird. In most cases it is estimated that there should be one bird per person but with such a rich sauce I suggest that half a bird will suffice. Most good game butchers will advise as to the length of hanging required and are well able to prepare and draw the birds as well. If you can't encourage your butcher to do this then try the local vicar! Serves 4.

2 partridges	*Sauce*
8 slices smoked bacon	1 shallot
2 shallots	1 chicken stock cube
4 oz butter	1 wine glass dry vermouth
	2 lemons
	2 tsp chopped chives
	1 tsp cornflour
	5 fluid oz soured cream
	Salt and black pepper

Wash the partridges thoroughly. Peel the shallots and place one in each partridge. Smother the outside of the birds with butter and place a generous knob on the inside. Wrap the birds in the rashers of bacon. Pre-heat the oven and cook in a baking dish at gas mark 8, 450°F (230°C), for 10 minutes and then turn down to gas mark 6, 400°F (200°C), for a further 20 minutes. Remove the birds from the pan and wrap in foil keeping them warm in the bottom of the oven.

To make the sauce finely chop the shallot and add this to the juices in the pan and cook until it is soft. Make the chicken stock to the quantity of $\frac{1}{2}$ pint and add to the pan together with the vermouth, lemon juice and chopped chives. Simmer until the juices have reduced by half. Mix the cornflour with a little water and thicken the sauce and season if necessary with a little salt and pepper. Just before serving the sauce, stir in the soured cream.

Heat a serving dish, pour the sauce on the dish and serve the partridge on top of the sauce on slices of fresh buttered toast.

Serve with crisp game chips.

Coffee Nut Cream   L.B.

The use of cream and curd cheese for making desserts is common in Eastern European, Italian and American cooking. The cheese counteracts excessive sweetness and adds a little sophistication. In Italian recipes Ricotta cheese is used, but this is not always easy to obtain in Britain. This coffee nut cream is easy to put together, and very self-indulgent. It will serve 4.

8 oz cream cheese	1 tsp instant coffee powder
2 tbsp condensed milk	(not granules)
2 tbsp Irish coffee cream liqueur	2 oz chopped hazelnuts

Mix all the ingredients except the hazelnuts together in a food processor or by hand.

Stir the nuts into the cream cheese mixture, reserving a few for decoration. Chill in the fridge and the mixture will firm up. Serve with boudoir biscuits. It is rich, and requires no additional cream.

French Mocha Ice Cream   J.E.

We all have weaknesses and I must confess that this ice cream is one of mine. I make it in large quantities and let it find its way to the bottom of the freezer where I 'discover' it quite by chance when there is no one else around and realise that I really must start to eat it as it has been around for so long. Then, would you believe it, as soon as anyone arrives it simply slips my mind that it is there and I offer them a biscuit! Serves 6.

3 oz castor sugar	$\frac{3}{4}$ pint double cream
8 oz plain chocolate	4 tbsp hot water
2 tbsp coffee powder	4 egg yolks

Place the water and the sugar in a saucepan and bring to the boil. Simmer for 3 minutes. Take off the heat and stir in the coffee powder. Place the chocolate pieces in a blender and pour on the coffee syrup mixture and blend until the mixture is smooth. Add the egg yolks and blend again for a few seconds.

Whisk the cream until it is thickish and peaks, and then fold into the chocolate mixture. Mix well and pour into a plastic container with a well-fitting lid and freeze for 24 hours until it is set.

Serve in dishes with chopped toasted almonds.

Lemon Egg Jelly   J.E.

A rich meal sometimes demands a more modest accompaniment in the sweet section and this nutritious recipe is well worth trying and very simple to make. Lemons are one of my favourite fruits and they are delicious in this light, refreshing pudding which slips down so well and provides a perfect end to a meal. Serves 6.

Rind and juice of 3 large lemons	$\frac{3}{4}$ pint water
	1 tbsp gelatine
4 oz castor sugar	3 eggs

Grate the rind of the lemons into a pan holding the water and sugar. Bring to the boil and allow to simmer for 1 minute and then leave covered to infuse for a further 10 minutes. Meanwhile dissolve the gelatine in a little water as instructed on the packet.

Whisk the eggs in a glass bowl and pour on the lemon sugar mixture together with the juice of the lemons. Place this bowl in a pan of simmering water and keep whisking until the mixture begins to thicken. Remove from the heat and add the gelatine. Mix well and pour the mixture in a 1-pint jelly mould. Allow to set and chill in the fridge.

Serve in glasses with silver spoons!

4 Take the Weight off Your Mind

I can't think why Lionel and the team have asked me, of all people, to write the foreword to this chapter. What on earth do I know about dieting, I ask myself? Well, I suppose there are some things I can share with you, and I have to admit that I am continually on a 'diet' – but not always a reducing diet. An important part of dieting is of course common-sense: if you are planning a baby and you feel you are overweight then go and see a doctor before you hope to conceive. In any event you should really go and see your doctor whenever you decide to make a special effort to diet; he or she is the only one who can tell you what is right for *you*. Just take the weight off your mind.

The trouble with us fatties is that when we start to have a thing about our weight we begin to imagine ourselves to be much larger than we really are! I know for myself that I tend to wait until nothing fits properly before I really begin to fight back . . . yet you can feel better in next to no time once you start to clamp down on the calories. Unfortunately, I am rather like the French who *live to eat* rather than *eat to live*, and I do feel Lionel is far better at looking after his figure than I am. The recipes that we have chosen are not in fact a 'diet' to be followed, they are little pointers along the way that might just relieve the boredom of dieting.

There are those of course who can eat and eat and never lose their shapely figures. I once went out to dinner with a ballet dancer and she ate far more than I could, yet the next morning she was at the 'bar' – the ballet bar – burning up all that excess energy. Sportsmen are supposed to enjoy eating a good deal of carbohydrate before taking strenuous exercise . . . but if you follow this maxim and the only strenuous exercise you take is to walk down to the car and then from the car to the office . . . well, you have only yourself to blame.

I do hope you will enjoy Lionel's 'Tofu Cheese Dip' along with my 'Eve's Veal Casserole', and please do not hold us responsible if you do not lose weight!

John Eley

Peter's Peaches   J.E.

This little recipe for a delicious and slimming starter was
dreamed up by one of the church choir who was also a
budding cook. It is very simple and if you can't cope with
the fresh peaches, do what I do and use tinned ones . . . but
those with no sugar added. Serves 4.

4 fresh peaches	1 tbsp French mustard
4 oz cooked chopped gammon or ham	2 tbsp freshly chopped parsley
4 tbsp low calorie mayonnaise	

If you are using fresh peaches these need to be very ripe and
you will need to remove the skin. The best way to do this is
to drop them in some boiling water for a couple of minutes
and then remove them with a serrated spoon before
carefully peeling off the skin with a very sharp knife.

Then cut the peaches in half around the middle rather
than from top to bottom. Remove the stone and place the
peaches on a serving dish. Blend together the mayonnaise
and the mustard. It is possible to buy some slimming
mayonnaise for those who are weight-conscious like myself!
Then fold in the chopped ham and half the parsley.

Spoon this mixture into the hollows left by the peach
stones and then sprinkle on the rest of the chopped parsley.
Chill well and serve. You can also use this mixture for
melons or leave out the ham and use some crispy fried
bacon.

Multi-Coloured Coleslaw   L.B.

Uncooked vegetables are not exciting in themselves, but
can be if they are presented with imagination. Though
British cooking has many good dishes to its credit, it is not
famed for its salads. What you are presented with can often
look very naked: a lettuce leaf, half a tomato, cucumber
and beetroot slices. In America, on the other hand, salads
can be almost too lush. Peanuts and pineapple pop up in

unexpected places, and you never know if you are eating a first course, a dessert or a side salad – or all three in one.

This coleslaw is very colourful, and appeases the hunger of those on a diet. They can eat lots of it without worry, even if they are counting calories with calculators.

For 4 famished dieters mix together:

$\frac{1}{2}$ small white cabbage, shredded	2 dessert apples, cored, thinly sliced and sprinkled with lemon juice
$\frac{1}{2}$ small red cabbage, shredded	
2 carrots, grated	1 stick celery, finely chopped

If the dieters are not too strict, take a heavy dry pan and toast till light brown:

2 tbsp sunflower seeds (you can get them in a health shop)	2 or 3 tbsp mixed chopped nuts

Add them to the vegetable mixture and make a low-calorie dressing by mixing together:

1 small pot of yoghurt (about $\frac{1}{4}$ pint)	1 tsp salt
2 tsp lemon juice	$\frac{1}{4}$ tsp pepper
1 tsp sugar, or a liquid low-calorie sweetener equivalent	

Pour over the coleslaw. Stir in and chill for some hours. The diet dressing can be varied by adding soy sauce, tomato juice, or Worcestershire sauce.

Mrs Proudie's Slimming Lunch   J.E.

Mrs Proudie, the wife of the bishop in Anthony Trollope's *Barchester Towers*, really ran the diocese and if she took a dislike to any up-and-coming cleric they would be diminished in no time after a few well-chosen words in her husband's ear. There are, of course, other ways of diminishing people and this slimming lunch dedicated to the Mrs Proudies of this world is probably kinder than any diminishment she herself could provide. Serves 4.

4 chicken breasts	Juice of 1 lemon
2 oz smoked salmon	Black pepper
trimmings	1 lb cooked broccoli heads
1 clove garlic	

In a food processor blend together the lemon juice, garlic, black pepper and salmon trimmings. Make into a thickish paste. If you feel it is too soft, add a few breadcrumbs, but this should not really be necessary.

Make an incision in each of the chicken breasts and stuff with the salmon mixture. It may be necessary to secure each breast with a wooden skewer. Place the cooked broccoli in a serving dish and keep warm. Cook the chicken breasts under a grill for about 5 minutes each side and serve on the bed of broccoli.

Remember: No wine . . . perhaps a little lemon juice.

Ceviche   L.B.

Food can be prepared in many ways, of which frying, boiling, baking and grilling are the most common. But there are other ways of preparing food which are odder, gentler and slower. The Dutch 'cook' their green herrings in salt, the Chinese bury their eggs, and the Norwegians inter their salmon with salt and dill. The ingredients keep all of their flavour that way.

It is not easy finding a food which is more delicious than Ceviche if you want to enjoy yourself and diet at the same time.

For 4 people as an hors d'oeuvre you will require:

1 lb fresh firm fish such as halibut (other cooks I know have used monkfish, plaice, sole and haddock), and enough lemon and lime juice to cover the fish completely (about 3–4 lemons with 3–4 limes). Make sure it is well covered and stays covered. You don't want to eat raw fish!

Skin the fish, bone it and cut it into chunks (1-inch squares). Put the pieces in a glass bowl and cover with the lemon and lime juice. The fish must stay covered with marinade – this is important.

Now add to the marinade:

1 seeded, chopped chilli if you like the fish hot and/or any herb whose flavour you enjoy. I like chives, thyme or oregano.

Let the fish marinate overnight in the fridge. It will become opaque as it 'cooks' in its lemon juice bath. Next day before serving, drain the chunks and serve them with sliced tomatoes and the greens of spring onions.

Pasta Salad for Slimmers J.E.

'Man cannot live by bread alone', but on a diet bread may be limited. So perhaps we can sneak in a little pasta and this light salad will serve some well as a main course. Serves 4.

4 oz Edam cheese	*Dressing*
4 oz cooked pasta spirals	5 fluid oz natural yoghurt
1 red pepper	1 tbsp low-calorie
$\frac{1}{4}$ cucumber	mayonnaise
$\frac{1}{2}$ head of celeriac	1 tsp French mustard

Blend together the mayonnaise, yoghurt and mustard to make a smooth sauce. Wash and deseed the red pepper and cut into cubes along with the other vegetables and the cheese. Boil the pasta shells in salted water, making sure they are not overcooked, and allow to cool.

Place the vegetables, cheese and the cooked pasta in a large bowl and blend together with the sauce by stirring very gently. Chill well and serve either as a starter or with a main course.

If you like full fat cheese but aren't allowed it, that's hard cheese! Cottage cheese is no substitute for a ripe and oozing Camembert, though it is nice in its own way if fresh. (If not, the curd tends to turn into gritty globules.)

You can make a sort of Liptauer cheese quite easily. Liptauer is a favourite in central Europe, and is very tasty. There is no standard recipe – every housewife and restaurant has her or its own selection of ingredients – so this version is odd but related.

I have used ingredients which contain less fat and fewer calories. Among them I include Tofu, which is now available in many health stores, delicatessens, Japanese and Chinese groceries, and in some supermarkets. It is a bean curd, with a silky texture, not too much taste (what there is, though, is pleasant) *and* it is good for you. These quantities will serve 4.

½ lb curd cheese	½ stick celery, finely
¼ lb Tofu	chopped
2 tbsp chives or the green	1 tsp caraway seeds
part of 2 spring onions,	(optional)
chopped	1 gherkin, finely chopped
2 tbsp chopped parsley	1 tbsp any fresh herbs from
1 clove garlic, crushed	the garden, if you have
(optional)	them (optional)
1 tsp paprika	Salt and pepper

Leave the Tofu in the fridge in its packet overnight. Puncture the packet and let any liquid drain off. Beat the Tofu and the curd cheese together, and mix in thoroughly all the other ingredients. Some people also add a finely chopped anchovy fillet or ½ teaspoon of anchovy essence and I approve. You might think there are already enough flavours. Pack into a presentable bowl and leave overnight in the fridge covered with clingfilm. This will allow the flavours to mingle.

As biscuits are out because they are fattening, serve with crudités – slices of raw apple, pear, carrot, celery and radishes.

Delilah's Veal Loaf   J.E.

The temptress Delilah brought Samson to his downfall by cutting off the source of his strength – his hair. She would fail miserably with me as I am bald, but if you do get tempted to try this veal loaf you can rest assured that it is not all that fattening and very tasty. I enjoy serving this in the summer and often offer it at cold buffets where it always goes down well. Serves 6.

1 lb minced veal	1 tbsp freshly chopped
8 oz minced beef	parsley
4 oz breadcrumbs	$\frac{1}{4}$ pint beef stock
1 tsp Italian seasoning	1 large egg
2 carrots	Salt and black pepper
2 Bramley cooking apples	1 onion

Grate the onion and the carrots into a large bowl and mix in everything else except the apples. Make the mixture moist but not too wet. It is advisable to add the stock gently.

Place half the mixture in a 2-lb loaf tin, then put on a layer of the sliced apples and then the rest of the meat mixture. If you have any apple left slice it on the top.

Bake for an hour in the centre of an oven at gas mark 5, 375°F (190°C). Then remove the loaf from the tin onto a baking sheet and bake for a further 15 minutes to crisp the outside. Serve with a salad as a delicious slimming dish, but if you are not on a diet you will still enjoy this loaf.

Lemon Mint and Pamplemousse Salad   J.E.

It took me some time before I had the courage to order a *pamplemousse*, my French being what it is I really was quite surprised when it turned out to be the humble grapefruit. There are some who say you should never serve it as a starter, and this recipe makes an equally refreshing and slimming end to a meal.

If you are not really interested in the dietary value of grapefruit you can cut them in half and sprinkle them with demerara sugar and toast them for a few minutes under the grill until the sugar is caramelised. Serves 4.

| 2 large lemons | 4 large grapefruit |
| 2 tbsp chopped mint | 2 oz diet sugar substitute |

You will need a very sharp knife to achieve the best results in the preparation of the fruit. With the knife peel off the rind and pith of the lemons and grapefruit. I usually do this in the bowl that I am going to serve it in to save any of the juices that may escape. It is a very 'juicy' operation. Discard the peel and remove the segments from each fruit by cutting down into the core of the fruit. Make sure that the pips escape.

Sprinkle on the chopped mint to taste and toss in the fruit. Sprinkle on the sugar substitute and chill well before serving.

Sheepish   L.B.

In my childhood, people became old before they were fifty, and were too worn down by work to bother about fashion. The older women, like my grandmother, had no figures at all. They were bulky beings, clothed in black padding and swathed in shawls, but had true hearts of gold, for their poverty never made them bitter. Their diet, like their figures, was bulky and consisted of potatoes, parsnips, flour and sugar, all of which were filling and cheap.

Modern ladies in their fifties are not like that. They are slim and fashion-conscious. With their children grown up, they are settling down to a new career or enrolling at the Open University. They eschew starches and calories, but will sometimes toy with unusual and sophisticated desserts. This recipe is both. Like the simplicity of high fashion, the ingredients have to be of the best. As this recipe was passed on to me without a name, but sheep's milk yoghurt is specified, I have called it Sheepish.

For 4 sophisticates you will need:

1 pint real Greek sheep's	¼ lb best bitter chocolate,
milk yoghurt (obtainable	preferably French or
in health stores)	Swiss
	1 hammer

52

Chill the yoghurt and the chocolate in the fridge. Put a cloth over the chocolate and hit it hard several times with a hammer. It will splinter into chips, if you haven't fiddled with the quality. Mix the chocolate chips with yoghurt and serve. Your guests will enjoy the chocolate, and the use of yoghurt not cream will make them feel virtuous. Few simple recipes can do more.

Eve's Veal Casserole   J.E.

This simple recipe for veal is one of my very favourite casseroles – and will not damage your waistline. There have been vast and humane improvements in the production of veal in this country and I do think that we can now enjoy it with clear consciences. Serves 4.

4 veal escalopes	1 tsp dried basil
8 oz Bramley apples	1 tsp dried thyme
2 onions	½ pint apple juice
1 red pepper	1 tsp cornflour
1 green pepper	Salt and black pepper
4 oz raisins	

Place the escalopes in an ovenproof casserole. Slice the apples and onions and peppers on top of the veal. Add the raisins and herbs with a little salt and black pepper. Pour over the apple juice and cover the dish with a close-fitting lid or foil.

Place the casserole in the centre of the oven set at gas mark 5, 375°F (190°C). After the dish has cooked for 50 minutes, stir in the cornflour blended with a little water and make sure it is well mixed. Cook for a further 10–15 minutes.

Serve with a green salad.

1 Iceberg lettuce	8 oz prawns
2 avocado pears	2 large red eating apples
2 large grapefruit	8 spring onions
2 large Mediterranean tomatoes	8 large dandelion leaves
½ cucumber	3 large lemons
8 oz cooked chicken breast	2 tbs wine vinegar
2 large carrots	Salt and white pepper

Find yourself a very sharp knife. This is essential and more kind to the vegetables.

Make sure that you buy fresh ingredients and that they are all washed thoroughly. If you are using frozen prawns do make sure they are properly thawed and that the chicken breasts are properly cooked. The dandelion leaves will probably be free. If you do obtain them from beside a path make sure you wash them well. I prefer to find a farmer with a large pasture who will allow me to go foraging. Farmers tend to look at me sympathetically when I ask for dandelion leaves.

The secret of creating any salad is to handle the vegetables as little as possible. When preparing the salad I like to put all the different elements in bowls covered with plastic film until I need them. Start by segmenting the grapefruit, then grating the carrots and slicing very thinly the cooked chicken breasts. Slice the cucumber and chop up the spring onions. Take the washed dandelion leaves, chop them up and sprinkle them with salt and white pepper and soak them in the wine vinegar for a while. Leave the tomatoes, avacados and apples until last and squeeze onto them the juice of the three lemons.

Now to work. Put a layer of lettuce in a glass salad bowl, then a layer of chicken and then build up layers of the other ingredients making sure you end up with a layer of lettuce. Sprinkle this with chopped chives. Cover with plastic film and chill well before serving. Make sure you have used all the lemon juice and vinegar on the salad as well. You don't have to be on a diet to enjoy this, so take the plunge. Think thin and you will not become a rabbit . . . I promise!

5 Unexpected Guests

If you can cook on board a boat, you can cook anywhere, for normal life afloat lurches from one emergency to another. Just as you are about to serve goulash, the cry goes out, 'All hands on deck!' A rugger team then hurls itself past you. One boot goes into the salad you were about to dress and your face goes into your goulash as the boat heels over.

As soon as you get to port and the crew are boozy with relief, invitations are issued. 'Come to dinner old chap . . . we (me) can always rustle up something. Yes, of course, bring your crew . . . and their girl friends . . . why not?'

'Why not?' Well, as you gently sip your gin, you could think of many reasons. It wasn't possible to lay in fresh food during the gale and there are no supermarkets near the Dogger Bank. Perhaps your guests will forgive you? You do have tins of course, but the good tin-opener went overboard with the garbage, and the only one left is a bad-tempered tool which always bites anyone who uses it. You had better get the sticking plaster out with the tins, and something to staunch blood, or make something with tomato juice so the gore won't show.

But necessity is the mother of invention (or is it the other way round?), and it's better than charity at covering a multitude of tins. You could drench the contents with akvavit or geneva and set them alight. If the guests look surprised at the bonfire, you can tell them it commemorates the Great Fire of London, or the time when the British burnt Copenhagen (unless your boat is in Denmark, of course).

Anyway, whatever you do, do it with confidence.

I like cooking for unexpected guests, because it puts me on my mettle, and forces me to try things which no cook in his right mind would contemplate. That is, after all, how mayonnaise was invented.

And the kitchen is just life in microcosm. Life never works out as theologians say it should, just as no recipe ever fits our kitchen or character exactly. We are always being stretched. Just as the meal is being served, there is a knock at the door. Who is it we wonder? Who wants something at this awkward time? My pious grandmother, without any learning, instinctively knew the answer – the unexpected guest is sent from God, a messenger who knocks on the doors of our hearts, and waits for us to invite him or her in.

Lionel Blue

Three-Minute Chilled Salmon Soup   L.B.

My unexpected guests rang the door bell. I let them in, and took their coats. In the few minutes before I gave them some sherry ('cooking' in a decanter), this soup was invented, created and in the fridge.

For 4 people, liquidise 1 7-oz tin of red salmon (bones, skin and all) with 1 pint of chilled milk. Pass through a sieve into a bowl. Add 2 tablespoons of chopped chives. Season and chill. Before serving add thin slices of peeled cucumber.

The soup is pink, and the garnish is pale green, and it looks and tastes fresh as a summer's day.

Curried Prawn Starter   J.E.

A quick and very tasty starter with simple and usually available ingredients. This dish also makes a useful addition to a cold buffet, and it can be created in seconds should I suddenly turn up to eat with you. Serves 4.

8 oz cooked prawns, tinned or frozen	$\frac{1}{4}$ pint soured cream
	$\frac{1}{4}$ pint cottage cheese
1 medium-sized onion	Salt and black pepper
1 tsp curry paste	Paprika
1 oz butter	

Finely chop the onion and cook gently in the butter until it is soft. Add the curry paste and cook for a couple of minutes, and then add the prawns and cook for a couple of minutes longer. Allow the mixture to cool and place in a separate bowl. Mix together the soured cream and the cottage cheese and fold in with the prawn mixture. Season to taste.

Place in ramekins and sprinkle with some paprika.

Serve with fresh brown bread and a twist of lemon.

Mocktail Cocktail   L.B.

Just because something is forbidden, it doesn't mean you just fold your hands, and do nothing about it. You use the ingenuity God permitted to you in order to find a substitute. When I visited New York, I was stunned by all the permitted substitutes used by my fellow Jews. They smoked slices of beef and fried them with eggs. They used milkless 'cream' for stroganoff, and did their best to break the shellfish barrier. (Shellfish is forbidden to Jews though not to Muslims.)

I got to like this particular attempt at breaking the barrier, and it was used in place of a prawn or lobster cocktail. It is also very quick and easy to make.

The 'prawns' and 'lobsters' for 4 people consist of:

½ lb cooked, firm, flaked haddock
¼ lb cooked, firm, flaked smoked haddock
1 or 2 small parsnips cooked but still firm, cut lengthwise in two, then into horizontal slices. (All the above should be cold.)

The sauce	1 tsp anchovy essence
½ teacup tomato sauce	Few drops of Tabasco
½ teacup mayonnaise	Salt and pepper, if
1 tbsp horseradish sauce	necessary

Mix the above, and adjust the flavourings according to your fancy. In the grandest glasses you possess, cover the bottoms with a mattress of shredded lettuce. Fold the fish (both types) and parsnip slices into the sauce, and divide among the glasses. This will be more than enough for 4, and could stretch to 6.

Double Time Taramasalata L.B.

The modern miracle of the kitchen is the food processor. It can do in seconds the work cooks took hours to accomplish in former times, pounding away with their pestles and mortars. The result is not quite the same, and if you rely on a processor too much, you will end up eating sludge in a startling variety of colours and flavours.

But some sludges are special, whether you call them paste, pâté, or poor man's caviare. This version of Greek taramasalata is a thick cream, which can be made in seconds in a processor. I have given quantities for 4 to 6, but it is very stretchable. You can bulk it out interestingly with curd or cream cheese. If the cod's roe is spread very thin, a little more finely chopped onion helps the flavour.

The colour is a pretty pink flecked with green. It is good eaten with Greek pitta bread, Jewish cholla or matzo, sesame biscuits, or just plain decrusted white toast.

4 oz smoked cod's roe	1 or 2 pinches of sugar
4 slices of white bread without crusts, soaked in water and squeezed dry	2 garlic cloves
	2 or 3 tbsp parsley
	3 tbsp chives
4 tbsp olive oil	3 tbsp double cream
Juice of a lemon	Salt and pepper to taste

Process the above, and if the mixture is too runny add more soaked, squeezed bread or cream cheese.

Smoked Gammon and Mushroom Soufflé J.E.

A few years ago there was a sort of soufflé phobia which really put people off attempting what can often be one of the most thrilling cooking experiences and a delight to all who are able to consume the results. The real beauty of soufflés is that you can make a little go a long way and this is often vital when you have a sudden influx of visitors. With this dish I sometimes add just a teaspoon of mushroom ketchup to give it that little extra. Serves 4.

6 oz smoked gammon	1 oz plain flour
4 oz mushrooms, finely chopped	1 oz butter
4 egg whites	½ pint chicken stock
3 egg yolks	Salt and black pepper

Cook the butter and the flour together for a minute in a thick saucepan. Pour in the stock and continue to beat well. Add to this mixture the egg yolks and gammon and mushrooms and adjust the seasoning with the salt and black pepper. Whisk the egg whites until they are really stiff and fold in the sauce mixture.

Pour the mixture into a 2-pint soufflé dish and bake in the centre of the oven at gas mark 5, 375°F (190°C), for 40 minutes. Remove from the oven and serve immediately.

Yankee Can Can   L.B.

Until I went sailing, I never respected my tin opener enough. Until I went to America, I never understood its possibilities. I only learnt respect for my tin opener when I forgot it after we were an hour off the Essex coast, and on the way to Ostend. Tins bend but do not break, and you can test this for yourself.

When I first went to America, I was snobbish about transatlantic food. Without any experience of it, I labelled it plastic, processed, and prepared. Well, a lot of it is, and very good too, if the cans are treated with American adventure and imagination. Americans are great improvers. They do not use the tinned contents as the canner left them. They sanitise them with dressings, enrich them with butter and cosmeticise them with plastic cherries and pickled silver onions. They are very good at dealing with unexpected guests, as they are an hospitable lot, and neighbours and neighbours of neighbours are always dropping in for a cookie, a doughnut or a highball. So when unexpected guests descend on you, drop your British reserve, put on your pretty pinny and get out your tin opener.

For 4 unexpected guests, take the following from your store cupboard:

2 tins of tuna, drained
1 tin condensed mushroom
    soup
½ green sweet pepper,
    seeded and sliced in thin
    strips
½ red sweet pepper, seeded
    and sliced in thin strips
2 tbsp butter

¼ pint milk
1 tbsp sherry (or more to
    taste)
2 tbsp double cream
Salt and pepper

Fry the sweet peppers in the butter in a saucepan for 2 to 3
minutes. Stir in the soup and milk and bring to the simmer.
Add flaked tuna. Add sherry, cream, and salt and pepper if
required. Serve on rice or noodles. That's it! There is no
need to hide the cans at the bottom of your garden.

Herod's Pudding   J.E.

I have always imagined King Herod as a sort of Roman Boy
George bedecked in jewellery and other finery but rather
gooey in the middle. I once read a book about his history
and came across this pudding at much the same time.
Somehow it reminded me of him – hence the title. Serves 8.

8 oz demerara sugar
8 oz breadcrumbs
2 tsp instant coffee powder
4 oz drinking chocolate
¾ pint double cream
1 wine glass rum

1 banana
1 large orange
1 pear
4 oz white grapes
4 oz black grapes
4 oz fresh cherries

Mix together the breadcrumbs, sugar, coffee powder and
drinking chocolate. Whip the cream until it is quite stiff and
blend in half the rum. Place half the breadcrumb mixture in
a glass bowl and then spread on the cream mixture and on
top of that the rest of the breadcrumbs. Cut the fresh fruit
into cubes and sprinkle on top of the mixture finally pouring
over the rest of the rum. Chill well and serve.

If you have no peaches you can use apricots or indeed tinned plums. For a real treat use fresh greengages, though these have become increasingly rare since I was a child. The first time I had this dish was in a rectory in Suffolk. It was cooked by the vicar who told me he brought the recipe back from China after the war. Serves 4.

1 large can of sliced peaches	1 tsp ground cinnamon
6 oz demerara sugar	10 fluid oz double cream

Draw off half the juice from the peaches and place them and the juice in a shallow baking dish. Mix the cinnamon with the brown sugar and sprinkle over the peaches. Pop under a hot grill until the sugar is caramelised.

Whisk the cream until it is really thick and then gently blend in the remaining juice from the peaches.

Serve the peaches warm and the cream chilled.

6 Exodus Eating

I am of an age when I still have very happy memories of eating excellent food on trains. Unfortunately, rail catering has been going through a sort of valley of death, and moves to improve the decline can only be for the better. I do not feel, however, that we can blame those in charge all the time because we, the public, have not really demanded the standards we would all like to sit back and enjoy.

Motorway service areas fill me with despair. The only really safe things to eat are baked beans on toast and possibly a little cheese. Despite the introduction of decent salad bars at some places, the general standard of motorway catering remains *appalling*. There is much I could write about this but I have now given up and taken refuge instead with the picnic hamper and a flask – except when I am in France where I really enjoy eating on the move.

It does not take much time to plan a happy *Exodus* meal, and we have tried to bring you a few tasty morsels that might make your journey a little more comfortable and relaxing. It is so much better to drive off the motorway and find a quiet lay-by to enjoy those delicious home-made snacks which really can make travelling a little more enjoyable.

Some of my travelling meals have been an occasion for parties and a great deal of fun. I once decided to travel overnight to my holiday destination in the South of France. This was when I was much younger and enjoyed the camaraderie of the crowded French couchette. At first we were all a little wary of one another but by the time we reached Paris we were chatting away merrily. Then we all began to feel hungry, and as the train was going to stand at the Gare du Nord for about an hour, some of us decided to go shopping for food. The choice was obvious: fresh bread, cheese and wine – lots of it! We had a super party as the night flew by and the holiday began. That is what *Exodus* eating is all about: whether on business or pleasure, eating on one's travels should be a 'little holiday'. And the best holidays have the taste of home . . .

John Eley

Cold Carrot and Orange Soup   J.E.

Eating on the move is always a problem and if you want to avoid the queues and the disappointment of commercial convenience food then take your own. This soup travels well in a thermos and is very refreshing if you are ever stuck in a traffic jam on the A30! Serves 6.

1 lb young carrots
1 salad onion
1 oz butter
1½ pints chicken stock
1 level tsp sugar

4 large oranges
¼ pint single cream
Grated nutmeg
Salt and pepper

Wash the carrots and grate them finely in a food processor or by hand. Chop the onion into small pieces. In a thick, large saucepan melt the butter and add the vegetables and a little salt and fry them gently for a few minutes making sure that you stir all the time. They are ready when they are soft. Stir in the stock, then cover with a firmly fitting lid and allow to simmer for an hour.

Ten minutes or so before the hour is up add the sugar. Remove the mixture from the heat and liquidise. Squeeze the oranges and add the juice and the cream to the carrot mixture. Heat the mixture through very gently, check the seasoning and add the grated nutmeg to taste. Allow to cool before chilling in the fridge.

This is an ideal and nutritious soup for eating while you are on the move. If you have your own chicken stock and you are used to planning ahead, leave out some of the chicken stock, about ¼ pint, and make some chicken stock ice cubes to add to the soup when you pour it into a vacuum flask for the journey. This really keeps it cool.

Green Pastures Omelette   L.B.

I was once on a train travelling across Europe. The buffet car had got unhitched somewhere between Florence and the Swiss German frontier. We had managed to snatch a railway buffet sandwich at a short stop. There was a lot of dry bread, with very little filling. Then two nuns brought out a basket. Like magicians out of a hat, they produced before our wondering and greedy eyes, cutlery, napery, a jointed chicken, fresh fruit, and slices of cold omelette, wrapped in paper serviettes with a pot of mayonnaise, which they proceeded to hand round. At the time it seemed like a foretaste of the bliss of paradise, for Peter Abelard said heaven is the place where you get what you want, and when you have got it, it is as delicious as when you still wanted it. I never asked for the recipe but this does well for 4 and is very similar.

In a frying pan heat 3 tablespoons of oil and fry in it until soft:

2 chopped courgettes
2 chopped leeks
1 clove garlic

Then beat together:

6 eggs	1 tsp salt
2 tsp cornflour, mixed without lumps into 1 teacup of milk	$\frac{1}{4}$ tsp pepper
	3 tbsp chopped parsley

Pour the egg mixture into the frying pan over the softened vegetables, and let it cook gently. (You may need another tablespoon of frying oil.) In the meantime heat up the grill until hot.

When the underside of the omelette is cooked, slip the pan under the grill. When the top side is cooked and browned, remove the pan. When the omelette is cold, serve it in slices and pass around a pot of mayonnaise.

Pilgrim Pies   J.E.

There is always room for a delicious vegetable-based dish in any travel food. Leeks are particularly good at holding their own against the onslaught of other flavours. If you wish to turn these pies into a vegetarian variety simply leave out the bacon and then honour will be satisfied all round. Serves 4.

1 lb leeks	½ tsp nutmeg
2 oz butter	1-lb pkt puff pastry
5 fluid oz soured cream	5 eggs
4 heaped tsp Parmesan cheese	Salt and black pepper
2 rashers smoked streaky bacon	

Roll out the pastry and cut out enough to fill four 4-inch flan dishes with lining and tops. In a thick saucepan melt the butter and add the nutmeg. Chop up the leeks into small pieces and season with a little black pepper and salt. Add to the butter in the pan and cook gently, stirring occasionally until the leeks are really soft. This will take 10 to 15 minutes. When they are cooked remove from the heat and allow to cool.

Now divide the mixture between the flan cases. Make a hollow in each serving of leek, just large enough to hold a raw egg, and then break an egg into each of the hollows. Place a dessertspoon of soured cream on the top of each egg and sprinkle with Parmesan cheese equally between each flan. Cut the bacon up into short strips and fry until crisp and sprinkle these on top as well.

With the fifth egg, which has been well beaten with a little salt, baste the edge of the pastry case and seal on the top. Prick 3 times with a fork and baste the top with the egg again.

Place in the middle of an oven at gas mark 7, 425°F (220°C), for about 10 minutes and then turn the oven down to gas mark 5, 375°F (190°C), for a further 20 minutes or so.

Remove from the oven and serve warm. If you are eating these on a picnic, wrap them loosely in a napkin and they will serve as a delicious and mouth-watering starter with a glass of good English beer or west country cider.

Thoughtful Lettuce Parcels   L.B.

I think the place where you need cheering up most is an airport departure lounge. Over the tannoy comes the dreadful news that your flight is delayed. As the news gets worse, the voice of the announcer becomes more and more genteel, until finally it is reduced to a squeak which is so thoroughbred and upper class, the message is beyond comprehension – which in the circumstances is just as well. The airport officials also hurry past, as if distancing themselves from your private tragedy.

It is best then, not to have to join the battered remnant of travellers around the buffet. Open your bag, for like the wise virgins you have taken thought for the future. While the foolish ones are morosely muttering over their desiccated sandwiches, you are fingering bright green parcels, stuffed with goodness. And if your misfortunes have not made you mean, you can hand them round, and be popular with God as well as your fellow men. You will need:

6 large leaves of a lettuce (Cos or Webb's Wonder)	Juice of half a lemon
	1 tbsp mayonnaise
A small 2-oz can tuna, drained of oil	2 or 3 stuffed olives, chopped
2 hard-boiled eggs, chopped	Salt and pepper to taste
1 tbsp chopped celery	

Blend all the ingredients together and chill. Put dollops in individual lettuce leaves. Make them into parcels by rolling them up, and tucking in the ends. Chill.

You can also use cabbage leaves instead of lettuce leaves – they are less frail – but then you have to cut away any hard root stalk, and boil them for a few minutes until they are softened.

Cornish Pasties   J.E.

Some of my most happy holidays were spent at Braunton and Saunton Sands in North Devon. There used to be a lovely old-fashioned grocery shop where every morning we used to go and buy our warm fresh Cornish pasties to take with us to the beach. Leslie Moon was the delightful Cornishman who had a face with the smile of the sun itself and always cared for our holiday needs. Eating on the move would not be the same for me without a Cornish pasty. If you want to be really complete, divide the pastry down the middle of the pasties and put the meat filling at one end and an apple filling in another. A really all-in-one meal. These quantities will make 4 pasties.

Pastry	Pinch salt
1 lb plain flour	6 tbsp cold water
8 oz lard	

Rub together the flour and the lard with the salt. Add the iced water and make into a good pastry but do not knead too much. Place the pastry wrapped in a plastic bag in the refrigerator for a while.

Now prepare the meat filling.

1 lb shin beef	3 tbsp cold water
8 oz grated raw potatoes	Salt and black pepper
4 oz grated turnip	

Make sure that you discard all the fat and gristle from the meat and cut the meat itself up into small cubes or strips. Peel and grate the vegetables into a large bowl and season well with salt and black pepper before adding the water.

Roll out the pastry so that you can make four 8-inch circles. On one side of each pastry circle place a generous helping of the meat and vegetable mix.

Seal the edges of the pastry circles well with egg wash and fold over the pastry sealing the edges well with your thumb. Turn the pasty on its back and brush well with beaten egg. Place on a baking tray and in an oven at gas mark 7, 425°F (220°C), cook for 15 minutes before turning down and cooking for a further 30–40 minutes at gas mark 4, 350°F (180°C).

A delicious and filling travelling companion.

Pan Bagna   L.B.

This is a sticky delight, oozing with tomatoes, which is eaten all around the northern shore of the Mediterranean. It's wonderful for a picnic in the Pennines or beside a pool with potted palms. If you are wearing a bathing costume the drips don't matter.

It uses up a lot of salad left-overs, so the ingredients for the filling can be altered according to your funds or fancy. But whatever you choose, you will need one French loaf, or *baguette*. Slice off a lid from the top, and scoop out the crumbs, so that you are left with a padded shell.

Mix the crumbs with some or all of the following or even more. Any left-over filling can be eaten with a spoon.

2 tbsp tomato purée
6 tomatoes skinned and chopped
2-oz tin of anchovy fillets (with the oil)
3-oz tin of tuna (with the oil)
3 hard-boiled eggs, chopped
3 cloves garlic, crushed
½ green chilli, seeded and chopped very fine
1 green sweet pepper, seeded and chopped
6 spring onions, chopped

½ cucumber, peeled, seeded, chopped, salted and drained
Grated celeriac, if you like its strong taste
Handful of chopped parsley
1 tsp chopped basil
3 or 4 tbsp chopped fresh herbs (thyme, rosemary etc.) or 2–3 tsp dried
2 tsp sugar
2 or 3 tbsp olive oil
Juice of 2 lemons
Salt and pepper

Season the mixture with salt and freshly ground pepper, and adjust oil or lemon juice. Pack the mixture back into the loaf, and replace the lid. Wrap the loaf in foil and weigh it down with any object to hand – an old flat iron for example. Let it rest in the fridge overnight, when the ingredients will amalgamate. Unwrap and cut into thick slices for eating. It is a sticky but substantial meal.

Kipper Quiches   J.E.

Children are very funny about kippers, but then so indeed are a lot of grown-ups. Some of the finest kippers I have tasted have been in the British Rail Restaurant Car, when the traditional British Rail breakfast used to be a luxury. However, it is not always socially desirable to cook kippers on the move – even if you heat them on the radiator as you drive – so here is a much safer way which children have been known to enjoy as well. Serves 4.

8 oz short pastry
1 pkt frozen kippers
¼ pint soured cream
1 large egg

Grated rind of 2 lemons
Salt and black pepper
Tomato slices to decorate

Divide the pastry between 4 small quiche dishes. Cook the kippers following the instructions on their packet. Strain off the juices and flake the fish with a fork. Blend the cream and the egg together with the grated rind of the lemon, and add salt and pepper as required.

Cook the pastry cases blind in an oven at gas mark 6, 400°F (200°C), for 15 minutes. When they are cooked spoon in the fish mixture and cook at gas mark 4, 350°F (180°C), for 20 minutes until they are set. Serve decorated with slices of tomato.

Povidl   L.B.

My friend Rabbi Gryn once asked his mother, 'What is your native language, mother?' His mother, in typical Jewish fashion, answered one question with another. 'Which one do you want, son?' And indeed most people from Eastern Europe switch from one language to another. My grand-father, for example, spoke Hebrew to God, Yiddish to his family, and English to his cronies, but he only swore in Slavonic tongues. (My Polish, picked up as a child, is in consequence hair-raising.)

In Eastern Europe then, nationalities were based on cuisine as much as culture. Every group and sub-group had its own flavourings. Fortunately a few recipes ran all the way from Riga to Trieste, one of them being Povidl. As the spelling of it is variable, I have given it in phonetics.

Now bread and jam might not seem much of a treat – certainly not fit for a cookery book, but if the bread is white, fresh and milky, and the jam is Povidl, you can serve it as a dessert with pride. It is rich so the portions can be small.

For 4 people you will need:

1 lb dried prunes
¼–½ lb sugar

1 tsp cinnamon
2 tbsp brandy

70

Soak the prunes overnight and simmer them for a very long time in a little water, till they are well cooked, and the water has evaporated. Take out the stones. In a food processor (or a mincer) chop the stoned prunes together with the sugar and cinnamon. Heat the mixture in a pan till you have a thick, sticky, dark mixture. Heat the brandy, set it alight and pour it over the prunes. (This jam is not nursery stuff.) Cook it gently for a few minutes more. Take it off the heat, transfer it to a pot, and let it cool.

You can serve it in little portions topped with whipped cream, or with slices of good white bread. It is excellent with Jewish cholla bread, and is a Sabbath treat.

Mint Dream   J.E.

This recipe is refreshing and delicious and certainly well worth making in small dishes for travelling food. It will always turn up as a surprise when most people might resort to tinned fruit. Serves 6.

4 oz butter crunch biscuits	1 oz castor sugar
2 oz butter	

Filling	1 sachet of gelatine
1 egg	3 tbsp hot water
¾ pint double cream	Green food colouring
2 oz castor sugar	1 chocolate flake
4 tbsp peppermint cordial	

Melt the butter in a saucepan and mix together the biscuit crumbs and the sugar with the butter. Press the mixture around an 8-inch flan dish. To make the filling, separate the egg and whisk the white until it peaks. Whisk also the double cream until stiff. Sprinkle the gelatine on the boiling water and stir in the peppermint cordial and leave in a cool place.

Whisk half the stiff double cream with the sugar and food colouring, stir in the peppermint mixture and fold in the beaten egg white. Spoon over the crumb mixture and allow to chill. Then pipe on the rest of the double cream and decorate with the crumbs of the flake.

The Mother's Union at our church have been singing the praises of these delicious treats for over twenty years and the recipe has been handed down rather like the oral tradition of the Old Testament prophets. Eta Clarke lives a reasonably quiet life with her husband who is 92 and still driving. It must be Eta's cooking! These quantities will make enough squares to feed 6 or more hungry children on a journey.

Base
5 oz plain flour
4 oz butter
2 oz castor sugar

Filling
4 oz butter
4 oz soft brown sugar
2 tsp golden syrup
1 small tin condensed milk
Vanilla essence

Top
8 oz chocolate block
1 oz butter

Sift together the plain flour and the sugar. Then rub in the butter and knead into a ball. Press into a Swiss roll tin and bake at gas mark 5, 375°F (190°C), until golden brown.

To make the filling, melt the butter gently in a thick saucepan and add the soft brown sugar, syrup and condensed milk. Stir continually over a gentle heat and add a drop or two of vanilla essence. Pour over the cooked and cooled base and leave to set and cool.

To make the top, in another thick saucepan melt the chocolate and stir in the butter. Spread this mixture over the filling and leave to set in a cool, dry place.

Cut into small squares about $1\frac{1}{2} \times 1\frac{1}{2}$ inches and enjoy as a really tasty treat.

7 Teddy Bear's Picnic

I have friends who delight in the 'Remembrance of Things Past'. They muse on their childhood, remember sentimental sayings of their nanny, and haunting little songs they sang with her. They cannot bear to be parted from the works of Marcel Proust, and take three or four volumes of his writings with them whenever they go to Benidorm, regardless of the cost in excess baggage.

I envy their delicacy, and would also like to be wafted back across the years, like the languid characters in Proust when they hear a bar of Mozart. I have conscientiously tried to refine myself by reading Proust. I've read him at home and on holiday, standing in a queue, and horizontal in a bath. I have begun those endless volumes, with their meandering trips down memory lane, in the middle, or starting from the end, and even from the beginning. But whatever the ambience (now, there's a delicate word!), or the technique, the result is always the same – I fall asleep. I would like to say it was a reverie but frank friends assure me I snore.

However, although I am too coarse for art and literature, my taste buds can still carry me back over the years. A spoonful of rice pudding, or a nibble of potato pancake (with apple sauce), and I'm back as a bouncy bawling baby, or a self-righteous teenager. I can even read a recipe as my friends read a musical score.

So what foods have the power to carry me back? I should like to answer you proudly with a list of delicacies, dishes with poetry and feeling: a perfect peach with the bloom still on it, ripe cherries plucked from a tree, and golden honey from the hive . . .

But, alas, my childhood in London's East End was not like that, and who could get honey in the Blitz? My memory foods are very different. I thoroughly enjoyed wartime dried egg. It had a cardboard taste you could stick your teeth into. I also liked peanuts. I used to crunch the shells while watching *Snow White and the Seven Dwarfs*. I then munched the nuts, and lastly used the bits left over as missiles on my mates in the cinema. Yes, peanuts were very satisfying, and they made a nice crackling sound during the performance. I also remember fish and chips, soaked in vinegar and salt, and eaten out of soggy newspaper sitting on the kerbstone. Before you gasp in horror, remember the dreadful things you liked as a child, such as bubblegum, and liquorice sticks and gob-stoppers.

In this chapter John and I have given a judicious selection of childhood favourites, robust enough to be honest, and civilised enough for adult consumption. We hope you enjoy their good taste, seasoned with happy memories.

Lionel Blue

Alien Corn   L.B.

My friend Tina is American, therefore she is not an alien here, but she is not quite native either. This is what she and her brothers were raised on. They used to have it for supper before they went to bed, with apple sauce.

There is quite a lot about corn in the Bible. The ancient Hebrews were attracted to the corn in Egypt, and Boaz was attracted to Ruth as she stood among the corn stalks. But their corn was different from Tina's, which is American maize and canned.

Here is her recipe for childhood corn fritters, which will feed 2 hungry children.

4 oz tinned corn niblets, drained	3 tbsp plain flour
	Almost ¼ pint milk
1 well-beaten egg	1 tsp salt

Mix all the ingredients together and let the batter stand for about 15 minutes. Heat a little oil in a frying pan. Stir the mixture and drop separate tablespoons of the batter in it. Fry the fritters on both sides until golden brown.

If you want to bother, you can separate the egg, beat in the yolk, whisk the white, and fold it in. This makes for lighter fritters, but at supper time or breakfast time you might not have the energy.

Sweetcorn Savoury Dip   J.E.

If you make food fun for children and give them surprises
they may eat almost anything. This dip is in fact excellent
for young and old alike and can be packed in individual
disposable containers for easy cleaning. It is delicious too.
Serves 12.

8 oz sweetcorn, canned or   1 shallot, finely grated
  frozen   1 tsp dry English mustard
5 fluid oz soured cream   4 oz butter
12 oz English cheddar   Salt and black pepper
  cheese, grated

Cream the butter until it is very soft and beat in the soured
cream, mustard, cheese and black pepper. Season with a
little salt. Use a whisk to beat this until it is light and fluffy.
Stir in the shallot and the sweetcorn and see that it is well
mixed. Spoon the mixture into a serving dish and chill.
  Serve with rusk-type biscuits.

Lemons in Egg Cups with Carrot Spoons   L.B.

All children, whatever their years, are addicted to magic
(religion comes later). Like everyone they want little pots
to put things in, books that open with stand-up pictures, and
blancmanges that look like rabbits. They like sausages
hidden in pastry cases, and anything stuffed with something
else as a surprise. So for 4 young or elderly children take 4
lemons and 4 egg cups. Cut off the tops, and scoop out the
lemon flesh with a sharp-sided spoon or grapefruit knife.
  Mash together:

4 sardines, drained   Pinch of sugar
1 tbsp finely chopped onion   Salt and freshly ground
2–3 oz cream cheese   pepper to taste
1 tsp lemon juice

Stuff the lemons with this mixture. Put on their caps at a
saucy angle, and stand them upright in egg cups. You can

make 'spoons' out of carrots, by peeling them and slicing them lengthwise so that there is a narrow end and a broad one. Children regard this as witty in the extreme, and you will be made to feel like Escoffier. You can use up the remaining lemon in dressings or salads.

Eggs 'Foo Yung' L.B.

Like very good French cooking, Chinese cooking is exacting and delicate. My own versions of Chinese dishes have no pretensions to any authenticity. They are strictly suburban substitutes.

These little omelettes are easy to make and consume, and they use up lots of bits. Children like them because they are colourful, and can be eaten with the hands. I like them hot or cold, or even in a sandwich, which is definitely not Chinese. As a picnic is a free-for-all, however elaborately you prepare it, I suffer little children to take as many as are good for them in the mêlée. The rest are reserved for me. This is not religious but realist.

For a dozen or more Chinese omelettes take:

6 eggs
1 teacup shredded cooked
  chicken
1 teacup bean sprouts
1 inch ginger root, grated
2 or 3 mushrooms, finely
  sliced
1 teacup of mixed, finely
  shredded vegetables of

different colours, e.g.
carrots, celery, spring
onion green, or leek rings
2 garlic cloves, minced
1 tsp cornflour made into a
  cream with 1 tsp soy
  sauce, and 3 tbsp water
Salt and pepper
Oil for frying

Oil the bottom of a heavy pan and fry all the ingredients, except the eggs and creamed cornflour mixture, for 3–4 minutes. Beat the eggs with the cornflour mixture, and add to them the fried ingredients. Stir and season. Oil and heat the pan again. Drop separate tablespoons of the mixture into the heated pan, and cook gently for a couple of minutes each side, shaping the omelettes with a spatula.

Serve them with a bottle of soy sauce on the table. Or wrap them up in a napkin and eat them cold outdoors.

Monastery Meat Loaf
J.E.

You never know who is going to turn up at a monastery and the monks are usually well able to cope with a few extra mouths to feed. I first had this at a monastery's open day, and the monks were handing out slices to the children who all ate it with relish. This meat loaf is a bit like a monastery inasmuch as it is filled with good things and can go a long way to feeding a good number of people, either in neat slices or in sandwiches. These quantities will feed 6.

12 oz brown breadcrumbs	2 tbsp tomato purée
2 lb minced beef	1 dessertspoon English
1 lb grated carrot	mustard
1 large onion	2 tsp herbs of Provence
1 clove garlic	2 eggs
1 green pepper	1 glass brandy
1 red pepper	Salt and black pepper
2 tbsp Worcestershire sauce	

Peel and finely chop the onion. Deseed the peppers and cut into small cubes. Finely chop the clove of garlic. Now mix all the ingredients together in a large mixing bowl. Spoon the mixture into a large loaf tin and press down well. Cover with foil and cook in the centre of the oven at gas mark 4, 350°F (180°C), for 2–2½ hours. Allow to cool with a weight on the top. Remove from the tin and serve in slices for sandwiches or in lettuce leaves.

A delicious tasty treat in the holiday heat!

Stuffed Apples 'Lord Woolton'
L.B.

During the last war, cooks had to become alchemists. Urged on by our concerned Minister for Food, they experimented with eggless, fatless cakes, meat loaves without meat, and economy pies with mysterious stuffings. It was especially difficult at a festival time to produce anything with glamour. These stuffed apples made a little meat go a very long way, and I remember them with pleasure.

Core 4 large dessert apples, and scoop out some of the

innards so that the apples are thick shells. For the filling you will need:

½ lb cooked mince (you can get by with far less)
3 tbsp sage and onion stuffing mix, mixed with 6 tbsp boiling water, the chopped flesh of the apples and some plumped-up sultanas
Salt and pepper to taste

Stuff the shells with this mixture, cutting a thin line round the circumference of the apples. Put the stuffed apples in a baking dish. Pour a tin of chopped tomatoes around them. Scatter over them brown sugar, salt and pepper and crown each one with a little knob of margarine. Bake for about 45 minutes at gas mark 5, 375°F (190°C), or until the apples are soft but not exploded.

If this recipe is too sweet – I have given it in the de luxe not the economy version – then use cooking apples in place of dessert apples.

Peasant Pancakes   L.B.

These potato pancakes are delightfully easy to make, and one cannot make enough because they disappear so quickly. The pancake mixture can be prepared in advance, and though the potato in it goes brown this does not affect the taste or texture. They are simple peasant fare, irresistible to adults and children alike.

Bearing in mind what has been said above, these quantities should be reasonable for 4 adults or 4 greedy children:

1 lb potatoes, peeled and   1 tsp salt
  cut in chunks   Cinnamon
2 eggs   Sugar
1 tsp salt   Applesauce (1 large tin)
¼ tsp vanilla essence   Oil for frying
3 tbsp self-raising flour

Blend the potato chunks in a food processor. Tip the goblet to drain off some of the potato liquid.

Add all the other ingredients, except the cinnamon, sugar, applesauce and frying oil, to the processed potatoes in the goblet and blend again.

Heat the oil in a large frying pan, until a trial slice of potato sizzles; the oil should be about $\frac{1}{4}$ inch deep. Gently drop into the hot oil separate tablespoons of the potato mixture. Let them spread, and flatten them as they are frying with a slicer or spatula. When they are brown and crisp on one side, turn and brown on the other side. Fry in batches. Lift them out and drain on kitchen paper. Serve hot, scattered with cinnamon, sugar and applesauce.

Chocolate Fudge Pudding   J.E.

There cannot be many people who do not like chocolate puddings, and this one will particularly appeal to devotees of chocolate. Children enjoy making it in the 'all-in-one' method and everyone enjoys eating it. Serves 6.

5 oz self-raising flour	*Sauce*
2 tbsp cocoa powder	5 oz soft brown sugar
7 oz castor sugar	4 tbsp cocoa powder
1 pinch salt	$\frac{3}{4}$ pint hot water
1 tsp vanilla essence	
1 oz melted butter	
5 fluid oz milk	

This is just so simple to make that I would even risk leaving children to do the mixing but I would keep an eye on them popping it in the oven.

Use the 'all-in-one' method to make the sponge mixture and place it in an ovenproof dish about 8 inches square.

Mix together the cocoa powder and the sugar and sprinkle it over the top of the batter mixture. Just before you pop the pudding in the oven pour over the top the hot water. Bake in the centre of an oven at gas mark 4, 350°F (180°C), for about 50 minutes.

Do not be tempted to look at the pudding in the oven as it is cooking, but allow it to get on with things by itself. The sauce will make itself and sink to the bottom of the pudding making a delicious 'gooey' substance which is irresistible.

This comes from my American friend Mervin, who is adventurous both in recipes and religion. It is disgusting and adorable, with transatlantic panache. British rice pudding is good but classical; this pudding is as romantic as MGM sunsets, with Dorothy Lamour crooning in a lagoon on a desert island, and belongs to the same period. It is not a dish for puritans, and I suggest you taste before you judge. It is a strange fact that children sometimes get snooty about it, but adults never.

You will need the following quantities for 4 people, but they will eat more than you think (or they think) and there won't be any left for nibbles.

8 oz easy-cook rice
4 oz tinned pineapple cubes, drained of their syrup and minced finely
2 oz blanched sliced almonds

Small jar of drained maraschino cherries
½ pint double cream, whipped
8 white marshmallows cut into small pieces

The method is simple:
Cook and cool the rice according to the instructions on the packet (don't overcook it so that it gets mushy). Fold all the ingredients gently together. Chill.

That's all! But here are two pieces of advice. Do make sure the pineapple and cherries are drained properly, and stick to white marshmallows, for I am told that the pink have a different flavour.

8 Comfort Food

There are times when you simply have to eat to build up supplies of fuel to go on. There are other times of panic and tiredness, when all the best resolutions about eating the right kind of food fly out of the window and you grab the nearest treat you can find, only to discover that you are doing yourself no good at all and just diminishing the resolve to be sensible about the food you eat.

At other times, though, you eat purely for pleasure, whether it be pleasure in the company you are sharing or in the fine flavours of the food. There is something especially comforting and reassuring about food we associate with happy memories: situations, people and places. For me it will always be the people who make the most important memories – bringing back those comforting moments spent and enjoyed in another person's company.

School meals are some of the memories that come flooding back when I begin to think of comfort food, but you will be glad to know we have spared you any such delicacies in this section, although at times I do yearn for chocolate crunch, or cheese and potato pie with baked beans!

There is yet another kind of comfort eating as well; when you wish to bring a little comfort to someone else. We often invite people to the Vicarage who are gradually turning the corner after some crisis in their lives, and tempt them with some delicious bits and pieces that will put life back into perspective once again. The recipes Lionel and I have chosen have their own particular memories for us and no doubt reflect our past. We will be eating them again many times in the future – when we need that little extra comfort.

John Eley

There are those smells and flavours of the kitchen which remind you of the comfort and security of home. This delicious country chicken soup is one such dish. It reminds me of wintry days in East Anglia and long walks in the snow and a general feel of well-being and comfort. It is also jolly good. Serves 6.

2 pints home-made chicken stock	1 tbsp finely chopped chives
8 oz mashed potatoes	1 tbsp finely chopped parsley
4 oz sweetcorn	2 tbsp single cream
6 oz cooked chicken meat	Salt and black pepper

I often sing the praises of home-made stocks and indeed there is nothing like the real thing for making home-made soups and gravy. So, on this occasion, I am not going to miss the opportunity of offering this recipe for a good chicken stock.

Stock	2 carrots
2 chicken carcasses (those from the Sunday bird will do admirably)	4 sticks of celery
	Salt and black pepper
Water	A bouquet garni of:
2 onions	marjoram, thyme and a bay leaf

Cover the carcasses with about 4 pints of water and add all the bits and pieces. Cover and simmer for a couple of hours, or until the water has reduced by half. This should form the basis of this delicious soup.

Having made the stock in a separate thick pan add about $\frac{1}{2}$ pint of the stock to the potatoes and make a thick sauce. Add the sweetcorn and the rest of the herbs and the finely chopped chicken meat. Add the rest of the stock and begin to heat gently. Never let it boil. When it is hot, taste and adjust the seasoning. Just before serving remove from the heat and spoon in the cream.

One of the most popular Jewish hymns is a numbers song. It goes back to a time when books were scarce, and a lot of information had to be learnt by heart. It starts off with the question 'Who knows one?' And, one, we sing, is the unity of God. Two are the tables of the law, three the patriarchs (Abraham, Isaac and Jacob) and four the matriarchs (Sarah, Rebecca, Rachel and Leah). You probably know the old English version of the same song: 'Green grow the rushes, O!'

I use the same device for remembering recipes, because I often don't have time to get my cook books down from the shelf before I begin cooking. So for this dish you will require:

1 clove garlic, crushed
2 onions, peeled and thinly sliced in rings
3 green pimentos, seeded and thinly sliced in rings
4 tomatoes, skinned and chopped
5 eggs, beaten together

You will also require the following ingredients which don't fit into the numbers game, but then no recipe or theology is ever perfect:

3 tbsp good-quality oil
3 tbsp butter
2 pinches of sugar
Salt and pepper

Melt the oil and butter in a frying pan and add to the hot fat the garlic, onion, and peppers. When they are softening add the tomatoes and sugar. When they have become mushy stir in the beaten eggs and season. Take off the fire before the eggs have set, and bring the pan to the table.

Letcho is simple fare, eaten all over the Austro-Hungarian empire that was. It is served with good-quality white bread and butter. This quantity will do for 4 as a starter or 2 as a supper dish. It is colourful, and much simpler than ratatouille.

Halibut is a delicious and strong-flavoured fish and served with this crab sauce is a dish that will please the most sophisticated palate. The dish is simple to prepare and tinned crab meat is recommended for the sauce. The best vegetable to serve it with is of course plain boiled rice, which complements the sauce so well. Serves 4.

4 halibut steaks	1 oz plain flour
4 spring onions	$\frac{1}{4}$ pint milk
1 bay leaf	4-oz tin of crab meat
Salt and black pepper	4 tbsp Parmesan cheese
$\frac{1}{4}$ pint lemon juice	1 dessertspoon tomato
1 oz butter	purée

In a shallow oven dish dot half the butter and add the bay leaf and finely chopped spring onions. Add the halibut steaks and season with the salt and black pepper and then pour on the lemon juice. Cover with foil and bake in the centre of the oven at gas mark 4, 350°F (180°C), for 20 minutes. The timing does depend on how thick your fish are but 20 minutes is an average time for an inch-thick steak.

When cooked remove the fish from the pan and keep warm in foil. Work together the rest of the butter and the flour and add to the juices in the pan together with the milk and allow to cook for a couple of minutes.

When the sauce has thickened add the tomato purée and the crab meat and heat through. Arrange the fish on a warmed serving dish and pour over the sauce. Sprinkle a serving of Parmesan cheese over each portion and fire momentarily under a hot grill. I have tried this dish with turbot and haddock and both fish stand up well to the flavour of the sauce.

Serve with fresh crusty bread and a good white wine.

Chicken Livers on Toast   J.E.

A little taste of luxury this, which goes well either as a starter or one of those really rich and scrumptious lunch-time dishes. Chicken livers are available now from deep-freeze centres and the like, but for the very best results use fresh livers and you receive the full benefit of all the flavours. If you want to be really wicked, serve these livers on fresh crustless bread which has been fried in butter. Serves 4.

8 oz fresh chicken livers	Salt and black pepper
2 oz best butter	2 tbsp double cream
1 heaped tsp plain flour	4 slices thick fresh white
2 tbsp medium sherry	toast

Melt the butter in a thick frying pan and add some salt and black pepper before tossing in the well-cleaned fresh chicken livers. Cook for a couple of minutes and then toss in the flour and mix well allowing the livers to cook thoroughly. Add the sherry and perhaps a little more black pepper and cook until you have a goodish sauce. Make the toast, and just before serving spoon the cream into the chicken livers and serve the livers on the toast.

Sprinkle with some freshly chopped parsley and serve immediately.

Budget Beans   L.B.

I concocted this dish many years ago when I was a student in Holland. Every place I studied added to the recipe. The beer came from Flanders, the garlic from Provence, and the steak and kidney from Darlington. Beans are cheap and meat is not, so their proportion was a barometer of my fortunes. This recipe has always given me good service because it reheats well, and is capable of transformation. Whatever flavours it started out with at the beginning of the week, it always ended up as curry.

Anyway it was a great comfort to know I could eat well and substantially on a small grant. It also has another comforting use. Sometimes, when I am anxiously 'cooking' a sermon, a reheated ladleful of beans does more for me than the conventional comforts of hot milk and biscuits.

For 8 substantial portions, or a week's supply, you will need:

1 lb dried canneloni beans	Salt and fresh ground
1 lb cut-up steak and kidney	pepper
1 can of beer	3 tbsp seasoned flour
2 cloves garlic	3 tbsp oil
3 onions, sliced	3 cloves
2 carrots, sliced	½ tsp cinnamon
1 parsnip, sliced	1 small tin tomato purée
Parsley	½ tsp sugar
1 tsp anchovy essence	

Soak the beans overnight, and boil them for 45 minutes. Drain and put in a casserole. Heat the oil in a pan. Shake the steak and kidney in the seasoned flour and brown it. Add to the beans. In the same pan fry the onions till dark brown and add to the beans. You may need some more oil.

Now fry the carrot and parsnip slices with the sliced garlic. Add the tomato purée and sugar. Fry gently a few minutes longer and add the contents of the pan to the beans.

Heat the beer in the pan, scraping into it all the succulent bits at the bottom. When the liquid begins to boil pour it over the beans with all the other ingredients. Adjust seasoning.

Put the casserole in a preheated oven, gas mark 4, 350°F (180°C). After 30 minutes or when it is simmering lower to gas mark 2, 300°F (150°C), and let it cook slowly for at least 2 hours. The longer and the slower the better.

When I was young and reckless, I added prunes and dried apricots, and this de luxe version went down very nicely at a party.

Fillet of Pork St Joan   J.E.

Rouen is one of my favourite cities in France and I have made several friends there in recent years. It can also be described as one of the gastronomic cities of Europe, and this dish comes from an occasion when a party of friends came with me to Rouen on a tour of Normandy and we had a final meal in one of the city's excellent restaurants. The food was delicious and we all left with a feeling of total well-being and fulfilment. Serves 4.

	Sauce
2 8-oz fillets of pork	1 oz butter
8 oz sausage meat	1 oz plain flour
4 oz chicken livers	$\frac{1}{4}$ pint stock
4 oz minced cooked	5 fluid oz double cream
chicken breast	1 glass calvados
1 egg	2 dessert apples
1 tbsp herbs of Provence	
1 glass calvados	
1 onion	
2 oz butter	
12 oz puff pastry	

A good relationship with the butcher is very important and if you can ask him to leave your fillet in one piece all the better. When you get it home split the fillet lengthways and flatten it a little using a meat hammer or a rolling pin. In either case it is a good idea to place it between a couple of sheets of greaseproof paper to complete the exercise. Now for the stuffing. In a thick pan or frying pan melt the butter and add the finely chopped onion. Cook it until it is opaque and soft, then remove from the heat and allow to cool.

Mince up the chicken meat and add the pork sausage meat, chopped-up chicken livers, onion, mixed herbs and beaten egg. Mix well and finally add the calvados. Some people like to add allspice and a bay leaf but these are optional. I always add a little more sage than is normally found in herb mixtures. Fresh herbs are of course ideal.

When you are satisfied that you have a firm, moist stuffing, cover the dish with some plastic film and leave it to chill in the refrigerator for an hour or two.

Roll out the puff pastry until it is 10 inches wide and about 14 inches long and lay the split pork fillet on the pastry. Spoon in the stuffing and then, if necessary, bind the fillet with skewers or string. I usually rely on the strength of the pastry when I roll it round the fillet and seal it well with a good egg wash. After rolling, turn the pastry in at each end and seal well. Place the roll on a greased baking tray with the joint downwards on the tray. Brush the pastry with a good egg wash and prick the pastry deeply with a fork. Bake in the centre of an oven at gas mark 6, 400°F (200°C), for 20 minutes and then turn the oven down to gas mark 4, 350°F (180°C), for a further 30 minutes. Baste the pastry with a little egg from time to time. To serve, cut into thick slices.

To make the sauce, blend together the butter and flour and add to the stock in a thick pan. Gently simmer until the sauce thickens and add the calvados and the chopped and peeled dessert apples. You may need a little more stock if the sauce is too thick. When the flour has cooked remove from the heat and allow to stand for a couple of minutes before stirring in the double cream. Salt and pepper may be added if necessary.

I sometimes decide to make small 'purses' out of the puff pastry and divide the fillet up into 6 portions beforehand wrapping each one up in a 'purse'. The aroma and the taste of this dish are quite splendid.

Grandmother's Liver Schnitzels   L.B.

During my vegetarian periods, I do not sigh for steak or roasts. They are too expensive for my family's kitchen. Instead I long for liver and lights, which were the meats of my childhood – when my father had a job.

The liver we used did not come from a young calf or lamb, it came from oxen which must have died of old age. My grandmother, whose ingenuity triumphed over poverty, managed to make elegant schnitzels out of dark ox liver slices. They were served prettily, and I have cooked them for a formal dinner party and not been disgraced.

As beef or ox liver has a strong taste, it should be sliced thinly and soaked for a few hours before use. On the continent it is usual to soak it in milk, but as this is against the Jewish food laws, we soaked it in water mixed with 2 teaspoons of vinegar. After the soaking, the liver slices are rinsed and very carefully dried. You will find that the strong taste has gone, or is diminished and acceptable.

For generous portions for 4 people you will require:

1¾ lbs ox liver, sliced thinly	1 lemon, sliced
Sunflower oil	A small tin (2 oz)
Seasoned plain flour	of anchovies
2 eggs beaten with 4 tsp	Parsley
water and 4 tsp oil	Salt and pepper
Fine crumbs (bread, or fine	
matzo meal)	

You will need 3 soup plates. In the first put seasoned plain flour. In the second the eggs gently beaten with the water and oil. In the third put the fine breadcrumbs or cracker crumbs, or fine Jewish matzo meal. Fine matzo meal makes the most even coating, but this may be childhood prejudice.

To prepare the schnitzels, dip a slice of liver in the flour with your hands, and shake off the excess. Now dip it likewise in the beaten egg, and let drip to remove excess egg, and again in the crumbs – making sure after each dipping and especially the last that it is evenly coated. Put it on a wire rack to dry out. Repeat this with all the slices, and let them dry for 15 minutes.

In a frying pan heat the cooking oil and lower the coated slices carefully into it. Do not crowd the pan. Fry for about 5 minutes on each side – until the coating is brown. Take out the liver schnitzels and let them drain on a hot plate, covered with kitchen paper. Keep the liver schnitzels hot and put a slice of lemon on top of each schnitzel, a rolled anchovy on top of the lemon, and a sprinkling of parsley on top of that. Whenever I eat them, I remember my grandmother's generosity, and how she could make even poverty cosy.

Gooseberry Fool   J.E.

My mother used to work on a fruit farm owned by the Rothschild family. One of the worst jobs was picking the gooseberries and I can always remember her coming home with extremely sore fingers from picking this fruit from its spiky bush. Since then, I believe there are varieties grown which do not have the spikes, and now you can happily pick your own. This gooseberry fool is a just reward for your efforts. Serves 6.

2 lb gooseberries	2 large egg yolks
4 oz castor sugar	$\frac{1}{2}$ pint milk
2 tbsp water	$\frac{1}{2}$ pint double cream

Clean the fruit and place in a large thick saucepan together with 3 oz castor sugar and the water. Place on a lid and cook gently until the fruit is soft. Remove from the heat and allow the fruit to cool. Make a purée of the fruit in a food processor or by passing it through a sieve.

The next stage takes a little more skill. Whisk together the egg yolks and the remainder of the sugar in a glass bowl until the mixture is light and fluffy. Add the milk and whisk again. Place the bowl in a pan of simmering water and gently whisk until it begins to thicken. Allow the mixture to stand and cool for a few minutes while you whisk the double cream separately until it is moderately stiff. Now fold the fruit and the custard into the cream. Pour into individual serving dishes and allow to chill.

Sprinkle some chopped nuts on the top and place in the refrigerator to chill well and serve with some *langue de chat* biscuits.

Strawberry Mountain   L.B.

This is really a case of making a mountain out of a molehill. If you have only $\frac{1}{2}$ lb of indifferent strawberries and 6 guests – then this recipe makes them rather splendid – the dessert that is, not the diners!

$\frac{1}{2}$ lb vanilla ice cream   4 oz castor sugar
$\frac{1}{2}$ lb cream cheese $\frac{1}{2}$ lb strawberries
$\frac{1}{2}$ pint double cream,   4 bought meringues,
   whipped till it stands in   roughly crushed
   peaks

First of all, hull the strawberries and cut off any bad bits. Dust with a tablespoon of sugar and leave to stand in the fridge for an hour. Just before serving, retire into the kitchen, and combine the slightly softened ice cream, cream cheese, and the remaining sugar. Fold in the strawberries and crushed meringues and, lastly, fold in the whipped cream. Mould into a mountain shape and bring to the table.

You could use curd cheese instead of cream cheese. This will cut down the calories but there are far too many in this recipe to eliminate them completely. In this world as well as the next you pay for your pleasures.

9 Loaves and Fishes

I had two shocks recently. I was shown the plans of a new synagogue. It was ingenious and multi-purpose. There was a big hall which could be converted into committee rooms and classrooms. There were catering facilities and washrooms, and there was even a 'worship area', economic of space but with all the liturgical basics. An ark would slide into the wall with a concealed lock, and a moving partition would separate the spirit of the big dance floor from whatever spirit cared to contract itself into the bijou 'worship area'. But what would happen if you just wanted to wander into a place of worship, and sit unseen in a corner, looking at an eternal light, and letting your mind drift towards eternity? Well you couldn't!

The other shock was of the same kind. A friend had bought a 'town flat'. It was beautifully appointed. Concealed cupboards and hidden wardrobes lurked behind every wall, the bathroom was carpeted and enormous with vanity units, and there was provision for a jacuzzi – when my friend had saved up enough. The kitchen was dinky. A partition slid away and, as in a dolls' house, there was a little fridge, a little microwave with a little spit for a tiny bird, and little cupboards for ramekins and such. My friend was enthusiastic. 'Why, it would clean itself!'

But such a kitchen would be of no use to me or John, because for us a kitchen is the heart of a household, a place where you have space physically and spiritually, where there are books and papers and recipes fastened to walls, where you can gossip to God and your friends.

I have never found it easy talking to people in my office. It is too clinical, too 'efficient' to be of any use, with its filing cabinets and sleek office furniture. My ministry is best accomplished in my non-purpose-built kitchen. There are no ramekins, and the wineglasses are sturdy, big and cheap, for people lose their grip on them when they lose their grip on life. The plates don't match, and why should they, because no two people are ever the same? The pots and pans remind me of my grandmother because they are built on generous lines and look ample and comforting.

The recipes for feeding the world should not be finickety, or tense. The cook must be able to relax, and enjoy his or her own party. A 'crumble' or a 'temptation' can stay in the oven a little longer, if the heat is turned down, and no ruin will result. Time will only help the vodka do its delicious work on the fruit salad, and make a community of all the vegetables bubbling up and down in a country soup.

If you say a kitchen prayer, and hand your worries over to God (who seems to want them), it is surprising how many loaves and fishes you too can provide. It is your own miracle of patience and imagination.

Lionel Blue

Spring Pâté   L.B.

I ate this pâté while I was driving through the English countryside. It was so lovely, I started to remember the Song of Songs, for the winter was past, the spring had come, and the voice of the turtle was heard in our land. The fresh green of the pâté matched the greenness all around me.

Make this pâté in large quantities and you'll find it is eagerly snapped up. And coming back to mundane matters – you can't taste the sardine, or the garlic – well, not much!

1 lb cooked spinach
  (fresh, or frozen,
  or tinned)
¼ lb butter
1 clove garlic, crushed

1 sardine (from a tin)
2 or 3 gratings of nutmeg
Salt and freshly ground
  pepper

Cook the spinach with the garlic. Press out the water from the spinach and garlic. Melt the butter and blend all the ingredients, including the melted butter, in a food processor. Adjust seasoning and spoon into individual pots. Decorate each with a twisted lemon slice. Chill in the fridge, and eat the same or the following day.
   Serve with toast.

Spritely Sprats J.E.

Living as we did not far from the North Sea in Suffolk there were always abundant supplies of this delightful small herring-like fish. Mr Boggis, our local fish merchant, used to go very early in the morning to the local ports and bring back the most delicious fish. They were very cheap and a few went a long way, but now they are almost a delicacy and well worth eating. Serves 6.

2 lb fresh sprats	Oil
2 oz plain flour	Lemon juice
Salt and black pepper	Parsley

Wash and dry the sprats. Coat them well with the flour seasoned with a little salt and black pepper. Fry in 2 batches in adequate amounts of oil or, better still, beef dripping. Place on a warmed serving dish and sprinkle liberally with lemon juice and chopped parsley.

Jansson's Temptation L.B.

I was first offered Jansson's Temptation in Sweden. It was the centrepiece of an elaborate buffet. Unfortunately I thought it was the main course and ate too much, but it was only a starter. What a starter! You can't stop eating it, and it contains more calories than I ever thought possible in a single dish. It is the antidote to any cuisine minceur. Incidentally, I do not know who Jansson was, or why he was tempted, and nobody in Scandinavia seems to know either.

For the cook, the ingredients are simple to prepare. It is a good-tempered dish which you can keep warm on a hot tray. Even if your guests dislike anchovies I doubt if they will detect them – they melt into the potatoes. This quantity will serve 4 generously as a main course or 8 as a starter.

1½ lb old potatoes	1 tsp salt
1 large onion	12 grinds black pepper
1 clove garlic	1 dessertspoon butter
2-oz tin of anchovies (drain and reserve the oil)	1 pint single cream
	2 tbsp tomato purée

Peel the potatoes and slice them thinly with a slicer, mandoline or food processor. Chop the onion and the garlic and fry them in the butter until soft but not brown. Grease a shallow baking dish. Mix the single cream with the tomato purée, salt and pepper. Take the anchovies from the tin and chop them roughly. In the dish spread first a layer of potatoes, then a layer of onions and anchovies. Repeat once more and put another layer of potato on top. Pour the cream over and shake the pan so that it goes down among the layers.

Bake for 30 minutes at gas mark 5, 375°F (190°C), covered with foil or any cover that fits. Then remove the cover, pour in the oil from the anchovies and continue baking for another 45 minutes or until the potatoes are cooked and amalgamated with the cream and the top is brown. If eaten as a main course, serve with a crisp green salad.

Saumon Fumé Tart   J.E.

When you are feeding a crowd and you wish to give them something special, it is not always possible to offer everything that you wish. This dish looks expensive and does make it possible for people to share the luxury of living at an affordable cost. The recipe is in fact quite old and originates in France. Serves 6.

4 oz smoked salmon scraps	Salt and black pepper
4 oz butter	1 lb salmon fillets
4 oz mushrooms	12 oz puff pastry
5 fluid oz double cream	1 egg for glaze
Grated nutmeg	

Mix together the smoked salmon scraps, butter, mushrooms, double cream and the nutmeg in a food processor. This should make a thickish paste rather than a thin sauce, so be very careful how much of the cream you actually add.

Cut the salmon up into strips about an inch wide and season them with a little black pepper and if necessary a little salt.

Line a 10-inch flan case with about a third of the puff pastry. Spread the paste on the pastry case and then arrange the salmon strips on the top. Seal on the rest of the pastry as a lid and glaze generously with the beaten egg. Bake in the centre of an oven at gas mark 7, 425°F (220°C), for 10 minutes and then gas mark 5, 375°F (190°C), for a further 15 or 20 minutes.

Make a parsley butter sauce in the following way:

1 lemon	2 oz chopped parsley
4 oz butter	

Finely chop the parsley and blend in with the juice of the lemon and butter when it is reasonably soft. Chill briefly in the freezer. When serving the pie place a knob of this butter on the top of each serving.

The Apostles' Fish Cobbler   J.E.

More humble than the previous dish and one for a family gathering, this fish cobbler fills and thrills. I always think of the scene in St John's Gospel when the disciples return from the fishing trip to find Jesus cooking them breakfast on the beach, and I can't help thinking how much they would have enjoyed this recipe. It is strange how fish prices change and haddock is now cheaper than cod in some parts of the country. You can make this dish with either or a mixture of both. Serves 11 or 12.

2 lb haddock	*For the Scone Topping*
2 oz butter	8 oz self-raising flour
2 tbsp oil	1 tsp baking powder
1 large onion	2 oz butter
1 large carrot	4 oz farmhouse cheddar
6 oz mushrooms	$\frac{1}{4}$ pint milk
1 tin tomatoes	1 tsp dried mixed herbs
1 bay leaf	
$\frac{1}{4}$ pint chicken stock	
3 sticks of celery	
1 tbsp plain flour	
Salt and black pepper	

First let us deal with the fish. Cut the haddock up into 2-inch strips. In a thick pan heat the butter and oil together and add the finely sliced onion, carrot and celery. Cook until they are soft. Sprinkle on the flour and cook for a further minute before adding the stock and the tinned tomatoes. Make a reasonably thick sauce. You can always add a little more stock if necessary. Place the fish in a ovenproof dish and sprinkle with the sliced mushrooms and the bay leaf. Pour over the sauce. As a variation to the sauce you can add a teaspoonful of mixed herbs or Italian seasoning. Adjust the seasoning of the sauce with salt and pepper.

Making the scone topping is blissfully easy. Mix together with a fork the flour, baking powder and grated cheese. Stir in the dried mixed herbs and then begin to work in the butter and milk and if necessary a little salt. Make a firm but pliable dough. Roll the dough into 12 balls, depending on your theology – it could be 11 – and place these around the oven dish on top of the fish in that excellent sauce.

Place in the centre of the oven and cook at gas mark 6, 400°F (200°C), for 30–35 minutes.

Cracked Wheat Salad   L.B.

Cracked wheat, otherwise known as burghul, is used widely in Eastern Europe and the Middle East. It can be bought in delicatessens, health stores, Eastern grocery shops and many supermarkets. It makes a very substantial salad, and has a nutty taste.

This amount will serve 4 people. It is not the sort of dish which requires precise measurements so you can put away your scales and measures and use your tea mug and kitchen spoons instead.

1 mug dry cracked wheat   1½ tsp salt
1½ mugs boiling water

Put the cracked wheat in a bowl. Pour in the boiling water and salt. Mix and then leave to stand for about 30 minutes, or until the wheat is chewable. Drain and squeeze.
    Then add:

¼ mug lemon juice
2 cloves crushed garlic
3 tbsp olive or sunflower oil

¼ mug chopped spring
onions and herbs, such as
thyme, chives or lemon
balm (mint is very nice)

Mix thoroughly, and then refrigerate for 3 hours.
Just before serving add to the mixture:

1 small cucumber, peeled
and chopped
1 lb tomatoes, chopped
(and skinned, if
you prefer)

1 red or green sweet pepper
(or a half of each for
colour), seeded and
chopped
½ mug grated raw carrot

Season to taste with salt and freshly ground pepper.
Garnish with onion rings, olives or more tomato. The use of
these grains is very old. Though such a salad might not be
familiar to you, it was probably a staple in the larders of
Nazareth and Bethlehem.

Mustard Glazed Gammon   J.E.

As a centrepiece to the table a good gammon can give
guests a real thrill. It is quite simple to prepare and any left-
overs are never wasted and very palatable. For decades, if
not centuries, this has been a popular dish in large country
houses throughout the land, sometimes with a cider sauce
and sometimes with this sauce. It is essential that the
gammon has a good soak overnight to remove the salt, and
that fresh water is used for its cooking. We are fortunate
today in that we can buy smaller joints than were customary
in the past and, scaled down, this recipe makes an ideal
alternative to the Sunday joint and does not spoil for being
kept warm for an hour or so. Serves 12.

7-lb piece of gammon
10 cloves
2 level tbsp English mustard
powder
2 level tbsp demerara sugar
1 lb prepared dried apricots

1 level tbsp tomato purée
1 tbsp cider vinegar
1 tbsp clear honey
2 tsp soy sauce
1 tsp Worcestershire sauce

Soak the gammon joint overnight in a large pan of water. In the morning remove the water and wash the joint thoroughly. Place in a large saucepan and cover with fresh water. Cover with a lid and simmer for 1½ hours. Remove the joint from the water and score the rind with a diamond pattern and stud the joint with cloves.

Make up the mustard with a little water and, together with the sugar, spread over the skin of gammon. Place the joint in a baking tray and place in the centre of the oven set at gas mark 5, 375°F (190°C), for 45 minutes.

Cook the apricots in a pan as per the instructions on their packet and add to this pan the rest of the ingredients. Simmer for 15 minutes.

When the gammon is cooked present on a large serving dish and serve generous slices with the apricot sauce.

Delicious with boiled new potatoes.

Rectory Rissoles with Love Apple Sauce   J.E.

If ever you wish to have first-hand advice at economic cooking look for a vicarage with a large family and you will find all the advice you need. One of my friends is in the happy position of having a family of six and his wife is well practised in keeping an eye on the family budget. Even something as simple as rissoles can be made quite stunning with Love Apple Sauce, and have you guessed what the love apple is? Well then, read on – you have been eating them for years, and some say this was what Eve gave Adam in the Garden of Eden, so anything could happen. Serves 6.

8 oz brown breadcrumbs   2 eggs
1 lb chicken meat (cooked)   6 oz mushrooms
8 oz smoked gammon or   1 tsp dried thyme
    bacon   Oil for frying

To make the rissoles, coarsely mince the gammon and chicken meat and mix in the dried thyme and some of the breadcrumbs. Finely chop the mushrooms and add to the mixture. Bind together with the beaten eggs used sparingly so that you do not make them too moist. They do need to be moist but firm as well. Ideally you should have a little beaten egg left over to coat the rissoles before you fry them.

Once you have made the mixture roll the rissoles into balls the size of ping-pong balls. Roll these in any spare beaten egg and coat with the remaining breadcrumbs. Deep fry them for about 6 minutes keeping an eye on them so that they do not fall apart. Use one as a trial and if it does add a little more beaten egg to the mixture until you get it right. Cook the rissoles and keep them warm before pouring over the sauce just before serving.

Love Apple Sauce

1 lb ripe tomatoes	2 cloves garlic
1 large onion	1 tbsp honey
1 tsp dried thyme	1 tbsp red wine vinegar
1 tsp dried basil	4 tbsp cooking oil
1 tsp dried sage	

Finely chop the onion and the garlic and fry gently in the oil. Add the herbs when the onion and garlic are soft and cook for a further minute, if necessary seasoning with a little salt and pepper. Roughly chop the tomatoes and cook these in the onion and herb mixture until they are soft. Add the honey and vinegar and cook through.

Pour this delicious sauce over those rissoles which have been waiting patiently in a warm oven.

Russian Fruit Salad   L.B.

I like recipes for food which looks after itself, such as fruit which makes its own syrup. This is a colourful Russian fruit salad, which graces any dinner party, and is as lovely to look at as it is easy to prepare. It does need a glass dish to show off all the glowing red fruits, and the vodka gets the company off to a flying start. Commercially soured cream can be bought in most supermarkets for ordinary pasteurised milk does not go sour, it just goes off.

The red fruit that I have suggested can be varied. So can the quantities but make sure you include berries, for they give it the fragrance of the great forests. For every 4 people I use 1½ lbs of fruit, using redcurrants and a selection of the

99

following: strawberries, raspberries, cherries or red plums, chopped up.

Stem the currants. Cut the strawberries in half, and stone the cherries or plums. Layer the fruit in the glass bowl, contrasting where possible the shades of red. Sugar each layer. For 1½ lbs of fruit you will need about 5 oz of castor sugar. Pour over 2 fluid oz of vodka. Cover the bowl and put it in the fridge overnight or for 3–4 hours.

Serve with a jug of soured cream. If you can't get it, mix together 1 small pot of plain yoghurt and 1 small pot of single cream (about 4 fluid oz each).

Sister Lucy's Juicy Crumble   J.E.

I do have a weakness for crumble puddings and, served with home-made egg custard, this dish really is nutritious as well as delicious. It is a family dish and heats up well if there are any left-overs. Pop one in the freezer for another day – it might give you time to go and pray! Serves 6.

Filling	*Topping*
1½ lb cooking apples, peeled and sliced	12 oz plain flour
8 oz blackberries	6 oz butter
4 oz honey	4 oz brown sugar
1 tsp cinnamon	4 oz chopped nuts
	1 large egg

It is always best to cook the fruit first so that it may cool a little before you add the crumble topping. So simply wash the brambles or blackberries under running water. Peel and slice the apples, and as always I recommend Bramleys which are able to hold their own against the strong flavour of the other fruit. Place the apples in a thick saucepan and cook with the honey and just a little water until they are soft. Stir in the blackberries and the cinnamon and replace the lid but leave off the heat.

To prepare the topping start by measuring out all the dry ingredients and stirring them well together. Then, using your fingers or a food processor, rub in the butter and finally stir in the egg with a wooden spoon. The mixture should be damp rather than wet with only the hint of an egg!

100

Spread the fruit mixture in an ovenproof dish and loosely cover with the crumble mixture. Bake in the oven at gas mark 5, 375°F (190°C), for about 50 minutes.

Serve with cream or a good home-made custard.

Home-made Egg Custard

6 large egg yolks	1 pint milk
3 oz castor sugar	1 vanilla pod

Whisk together the eggs and the sugar in a large glass bowl until they are light and fluffy. If you are using vanilla essence instead of a vanilla pod add it at this point. If you are using a vanilla pod heat the milk with the vanilla pod in it and leave it to infuse for a good 10 minutes and then add the milk to the egg mixture and stir well. Pour the whole mixture into a double boiler and stir gently until the back of a spoon will be coated with the custard. Don't be tempted to leave it too long on the heat at this stage.

Leave it to stand for about 10 minutes before serving with Sister Lucy's Juicy Crumble.

10 Putting on the Style

Lonnie Donegan used to have a song which went something like this: 'Putting on the agony, putting on the style . . . that's what the young folk are doing all the while . . .'

When it comes to cooking, both Lionel and I would agree that a little bit of style is fine, but agony is definitely out. If you have a disaster, you just have to be bold enough to call the dish by a new name. A flattened soufflé can become 'Tacky Omelette' . . . or something like that! There are occasions, though, when you do want to be at your best, especially when entertaining the in-laws or a prospective lover. Then you must pull out all the stops, but the real secret to success is simply to relax and enjoy what you are doing. After all, cooking is really an escape into a world of fantasy and creativity – and that must be good for you, as well as for recipients of your loving labours. Stir a little love in and then you are sure to have the success you deserve.

Here are a few tips which may help, and I hope that you will try them. I usually like to get the table set and out of the way first. Then, if nothing else works, at least what you have prepared will benefit from a stylish setting. Then to cooking: the enjoyment must come from the moment you buy the first Brussels sprout right through until the moment you sit down and enjoy your meal. Remember, you are to spoil yourself as well as your guests . . . that really is style.

Sometimes it is fun to have a theme running through a meal: an all-white meal for example, with chicken soup, a cauliflower vegetable with fish, and perhaps some vanilla ice cream. Or you can let your hair down and serve everything flambé like a gastronomic 'Dante's Inferno'. This should be fun!

Together, Lionel and I have chosen some recipes to act as coat-hangers, upon which you can hang your culinary laurels with safety, while not ruining your purse. They are invitations to you to put on the style!

John Eley

Company Cucumber Soup   L.B.

Stylish cooking does not have to be expensive cooking. If your guests are businessmen they will probably be grateful for a break in the monotony of expense-account lunches, with their fixed procession of prawn cocktail, sole, and any fruit that is out of season.

This soup hails from the Balkans and the Middle East, and it is very cooling and refreshing on a hot day. For 4 tired businessmen you will require:

2 peeled, seeded and chopped cucumbers	1 tbsp dill
2 tbsp chives	$\frac{1}{2}$ pint single cream
2 tbsp chopped fresh mint (optional)	$\frac{1}{2}$ pint best-quality yoghurt
2 tbsp chopped fresh parsley	Salt and white pepper
	Pinch of sugar to taste

Salt the cucumber in a colander. Let it stand for an hour, then rinse it through, drain it and let it dry.

Blend all the ingredients together in a food processor, and let the mixture chill in the fridge. Serve in bowls. If you want to make this refreshing starter a little more grand, then add 2 oz of chopped walnuts.

Avocado Soup   L.B.

Salmon was once so cheap, that it was written into servants' contracts that they should not have too much of it. Herrings, which in my childhood were almost give-away, are still inexpensive but certainly not for the taking and trout is still a treat, but affordable if you have a job. Avocados, if you buy them when they are ripe and being sold off, are not only cheap, but also nutritious and very versatile. It is simple to turn them into an hors d'oeuvre, a soup, a dip or a dessert.

Here is a recipe for thick, chilled avocado soup, filling enough to require only good bread and fruit for a summer lunch. It will serve 4 generously.

1 large ripe avocado
½ pint hot vegetable stock (it can be made with a cube)
¾ pint milk
4 oz single cream
2 tsp salt
12 grinds pepper

2 oz dried potato flakes or 4 oz left-over skinned baked potatoes
2 spring onions
1 tbsp lemon juice (or more to taste)
Chopped chives

Mix the hot stock with the potato flakes. Chop the spring onions, and scoop out the flesh of the avocado. In a blender or a food processor mix all the ingredients except the cream and lemon juice. When the mixture is well blended, stir in the cream, and then the lemon juice. Chill thoroughly for 2–3 hours.

Serve garnished with chopped chives.

Pork Chops Inferno   J.E.

I am always looking for ways of doing something different with the gallant pork chop and this dish is one which recently came into my hands. The sauce is delicious and full of spices, and helps to keep the chops moist and luscious. Serves 4.

4 loin pork chops
1 English onion
2 large cooking apples
2 tbsp oil
1 chicken stock cube
2 tbsp honey

1 tbsp cider vinegar
1 tbsp Worcestershire sauce
1 dash of Tabasco
2 oz seedless raisins
Salt and black pepper
A little sherry

In a thick oven dish heat the oil and gently fry the sliced onion, together with the sliced and peeled apples. Bramleys are really the very best for this sort of dish. Cook them together gently until they are both very soft. It is a good idea to add the apples after having cooked the onions for a while.

Add the rest of the ingredients and have a little sherry standing by . . . just in case! Cook the sauce gently for a minute or so before adding the chops. Make sure that you cover the chops well with the delicious sauce: it really is spicy! Adjust the amount of sauce you desire by adding a little sherry.

Place the dish in the oven set at gas mark 5, 375°F (190°C), and allow to cook for about 40 minutes or until the chops are done.

Serve with potatoes baked in their jackets.

Spiked Barnsley Chops   J.E.

We have the best lamb in the world in this country with regional variations in flavour and style, and the sight of a tray of double or butterfly chops is very pleasing to the eye. They are now becoming increasingly available much to the joy of both farmers and butchers, although sometimes you will have to order them in advance as many butchers split their carcasses on arrival from the slaughterhouse. There is a difference between the Herdwick and the Blue Faced Leicester, but both have benefited from being crossed with the Suffolk. However, I am biased because my father looked after a flock of splendid Suffolks for many years and they were exported all over the world. Serves 4.

4 Barnsley chops, also called butterfly lamb chops	8 oz white cabbage
	5 fluid oz milk
	2 oz raisins
1 onion	1 tbsp Worcestershire sauce
1 clove garlic	Salt and black pepper
3 carrots	

Trim the fat off the chops and season well with salt and black pepper. Heat some oil in a thick frying pan. Brown the chops on each side and turn down the heat until they are cooked. Remove from the pan and keep warm. Finely slice the onion and chop up the garlic and cook in the juices left by the chops until they are soft. Slice the carrots and the cabbage and add to the pan together with the milk and Worcestershire sauce. Simmer for 5 minutes. Stir frequently and cook until the juices are almost used up. Add the raisins and heat through. Place the chops on a heated serving dish and spoon over the vegetable mixture.

Serve with well-buttered baked potatoes.

Fennel and Anchovy Salad   L.B.

If you have gone native in Provence or Italy and enjoyed the
aniseed taste in Pernod, or Ricard, then you would like the
same taste in a solid form too. Now you are in the Common
Market, you might as well enjoy its delights. For 4 people
you will need:

2 fennel bulbs
2-oz tin anchovy fillets in
  olive oil
12 leaves radicchio
4 tbsp chopped parsley

Dressing
10 tbsp olive oil (using oil
  from the anchovy tin,
  topped up with olive oil)
5 tbsp cider vinegar
1 tsp sugar
1 tsp salt
12 grinds of fresh ground
  pepper
$\frac{1}{4}$ tsp mustard powder

Mix all the ingredients for the dressing in a liquidiser or in a
screw-top jar. Cut off and discard the roots and tops of the
fennel bulbs, wash them, and slice them thinly on a slicer or
on a mandoline. Turn them in the dressing so that they do
not discolour. Leave them in the fridge to chill for an hour.

Lay the radicchio leaves on a platter or on individual
plates, and pile the dressed fennel on top. Halve the
anchovy fillets into thinner strips and arrange them criss-
cross over the fennel. Scatter with chopped parsley.

St David's Pie   J.E.

The Welsh really do know how to get the best out of their
lamb and this dish is one of their finest. I have been
practising making this dish to celebrate a friend's appoint-
ment as organist of St Asaph's Cathedral, although he is
also a good cook and I am rather sticking my neck out
feeding him his native cuisine. Being a pie, I suppose, this is
the sort of dish that he could take up to the organ loft and
keep warm for eating during the sermon! Serves 6.

1½ lb lamb meat cut into
  1-inch cubes
2 oz flour
Salt and black pepper
½ tsp dried thyme
½ tsp dried rosemary
4 lamb's kidneys

1½ lb leeks
1½ lb potatoes, peeled and
  sliced
1 pint good chicken stock
5 fluid oz soured cream
12 oz puff pastry
1 egg, well beaten

Toss the cubed lamb in the flour, salt and pepper making sure that it is all well coated. Trim and core the kidneys, cut these up into smallish pieces and add to the meat. Place the meat in a buttered dish and sprinkle on the dried herbs. Then layer the dish with alternate layers of chopped leeks and sliced potatoes until it is full. Pour on the stock and add a little more salt and pepper. Cover the dish and bake in the oven at gas mark 5, 375°F (190°C), for about 1½ hours. When it is cooked remove from the oven and allow to cool.

In the meantime roll out the puff pastry in a large enough piece to cover the dish, allowing extra for strips to form a seal around the edge, basted well with the beaten egg. Just before placing the pastry lid on the dish, spoon on the soured cream and then seal on the pastry lid, making sure you have left some holes for the steam to escape. Baste the pastry lid well with the beaten egg and cook in the oven at gas mark 7, 425°F (220°C), for 10 minutes and then turn the oven down to gas mark 5, 375°F (190°C), for 20 minutes.

Serve with root vegetables on a cold winter's day.

Hare Casserole   J.E.

Several years ago Hare Coursing was a sport of the landed gentry and farmers in this country. It entailed dogs chasing and catching hares for sport, but fortunately those days are over and hares are now killed more humanely. At certain times of the year, from September to February, hare is even available in some supermarkets. It is a dark rich meat and is not to be confused with the lighter meat of the rabbit. It does make very stylish dishes and is well worth a try. Serves 4.

4 hare joints	3 tbsp flour
4 shallots	¾ pint beef stock
1 medium carrot cut into	1 bouquet garni
strips	Salt and black pepper
1 oz butter	6 fluid oz port
1 tbsp olive oil	4 oz cranberry sauce

Heat the butter and oil in a thick cast-iron casserole and brown the hare joints well. Remove the joints from the pan and add the chopped shallots and the strips of carrot and cook for 5 minutes. Sift in the flour and cook for a further minute and blend in the stock.

Return the meat to the casserole and add the bouquet garni and season. Cover the casserole with a tight-fitting lid and cook in the oven at gas mark 3, 325°F (170°C), for 2 hours.

After cooking remove the joints from the casserole and keep warm. Strain off 1 pint of the sauce into a thick saucepan. Add the port and cranberry sauce and simmer for about 5 minutes. Return the joint to the casserole and pour on this excellent sauce and cover and simmer in the oven for a further 20 minutes. Adjust the seasoning.

Serve with mashed potato and swede.

Ostentatious Fruit   L.B.

When your guests taste this, they will know you are putting on the style – even if they had their doubts before – for the aroma of the wild strawberries is quite convincing. They will also feel pleased that you have not bulldozed them with whipped cream and pastry, and respected their subtlety and their figures. This dish is simple but not cheap, and if you don't know whether you can afford it, then you can't. For 4 adequate portions, you will require:

1 lb fresh raspberries	1 tbsp icing sugar
1 lb wild strawberries	1 tbsp Curaçao or Cointreau
(ordinary ones will	1 tsp lemon juice
not do)	

Process all the ingredients except the raspberries. Let the mixture stand for an hour. Divide the raspberries into 4 glasses. Sieve the wild strawberry mixture, and pour it equally over the raspberry portions. It does not need any cream. It is not cheap but it is not vulgar either!

Stella Fruit Pie   J.E.

There are several ways of making a plain fruit pie into something rather special and this is certainly one of them. Red or green plums are delicious served this way and make a grand accompaniment to a game main course. I used to love the rich Victoria plums we were able to 'scrump' from certain orchards when we were young. Now I have my own tree in the Vicarage garden but have a constant battle with insects who seem to enjoy the plums as much as we do. I must have a word with Alan Titchmarsh! Serves 6.

Filling
1½ lb plums
6 oz castor sugar
A little water
1 tsp cinnamon

Top
1 pkt puff pastry
4 oz castor sugar
2 lemons
Spare sugar for sprinkling
1 beaten egg

Wash the plums and place them in a thick saucepan with the water, sugar and cinnamon. Cover with a tight-fitting lid and simmer for 30 minutes or until the plums are cooked.

Take the puff pastry and roll out into a rectangle 14 × 10 inches. Sprinkle on the castor sugar, the squeezed lemon juice, and the grated rind of the lemons. Brush the edge of the pastry with the beaten egg. Roll the pastry similar to a Swiss roll and cut into slices. Arrange these on top of the fruit which has been placed in a shallow, round baking dish. Brush with the beaten egg and cook in the oven at gas mark 7, 425°F (220°C), for 40 minutes. Serve with sugar and cream . . . of course.

It took me a long time to realise that true elegance is very simple, whether it is found in food, fashion, clothes or sermons. My first sermons were very complicated. They were loaded with learning, and collapsed under the weight of quotations. My congregation nearly collapsed too, because they lasted far too long. People tottered away after the service, wondering if their lunch was burnt. It takes a lot of experience to make a simple point simply, using the right illustration with an ending which is clear cut, and doesn't fade away into a mumble.

It is the same with food. Nothing complicated is needed for a perfect party dish, but the ingredients must be well chosen. This elegant fruit salad is a fine example, for it does not even require exact quantities.

You will need those green-fleshed, aromatic Ogen melons. They can sometimes be quite inexpensive when they are ripe. Cut them carefully in half, and scoop out the flesh with a melon baller. Put the balls and the juice in a glass dish.

You will need the same quantity of stoned sweet black cherries as of melon. A cherry stoner is a handy little gadget, and will do the job neatly. Mix the cherries with the melon. Sprinkle some appropriate liqueur over the fruit, such as Kirsch, Curaçao or Maraschino. Chill.

You can serve the salad from the bowl, or in the melon shells, if they are unblemished and you have enough of them. Unlike John's final recipe, I urge no cream please, and no sugar!